George

Mafia, Manchuria, and... North Carolina

Roland Woody

the Peppertree Press
Sarasota, Florida

Graphic design by Rebecca Barbier.

For information regarding permission,
call 941-922-2662 or contact us at our website:
www.peppertreepublishing.com or write to:
the Peppertree Press, LLC.
Attention: Publisher
1269 First Street, Suite 7
Sarasota, Florida 34236

ISBN: 978-1-61493-172-0

Library of Congress Number: 2013905161

Printed in the U.S.A.

Printed April 2013

For my best friend

The thoughts, feelings, and untold stories of my best friend's life that I have held within me for over forty years might never have made it to the page without the help of Robert Van Praag. I do not thank you merely for the words, but for the guidance, patience, and concern you put into a person's life that is precious to me.

Prologue

"What is a friend?
A single soul dwelling in two bodies."
~Aristotle~

Long before the resolutions are made that will be forgotten by the end of the week, or more than likely never make their way through the fog of the next day's hangover, rooms are filled with laughter. Before the glass of champagne is raised, where a plastic cork makes no difference since it was preceded by three or five drinks, on New Year's Eve party goers—be they wearing hats or intent on deafening all within a mile with dime store noise makers, don their smiles and sneers as they reminisce about the year that has passed.

While personal tales of happiness and woes are shared between friends and loved ones and—more often than not, with a mirror, reflections of the year, be they good or bad, as it pertains to the world we live in overwhelm a crowded room until the first couple of drinks take their effect. In some cases the smiles turn into sneers and the sneers into smiles.

Few, if any, think that New Year's Eve itself will actually be the night that is filled with the most important revelation of the year that has passed.

Of those few that might exist there have been thought to be one or two individuals that might come to the conclusion of the previous year's revelation three hundred and sixty five nights from the day of inception.

Others, like me, would wait years to come to terms with the fact that it was the most important night of their lives. It would be a night, a person, which would hold the power of transformation, enlightenment.

With the smiles broadening as the jokes worsened the reminiscences on New Years Eve 1961 were no different. It was a year when the threat of communism sent the world into frenzy, when John Kennedy took responsibility for The Bay of Pigs, and the erection of the Berlin Wall began. It was a year when within the DMZ of Korea snipers who had never fired a weapon before were on alert for the enemy and a year when masses in Brussels were hording rations sure that the world was about to embark on another epic war.

If any of these events were going through my head on New Year's Eve 1961 either I have no recall or they paled in remembrance to the night itself.

I lie. It wasn't that they paled nor was it the night. It was a person.

For me, New Year's Eve 1961 was the night that changed my life, only I didn't know it at the time. Hence, I should say *would eventually* change my life. It would take me years to begin to see, to feel, the effects of that night and well over a decade to truly recognize the impact.

The impact, that is, which one human being can have upon another.

I was at a private party being held in the basement of a restaurant in Asheville, North Carolina. It was a typical New Year's Eve party, as far as I was concerned, where the room was crowded, the bar was more crowded, and I was *sipping* my bourbon.

Over the music and all too familiar, I say with expertise, pick-up lines I heard recognizable laughter. Turning to greet the friend whose laughter could be heard in Boise, I saw the giant he had with him. The fifty years that have passed since I first met George Wilson *might* have me exaggerating over the term "giant," but at the age of thirty, and with a few drinks in me, I was overwhelmed by his physical presence. Now, without embellishment, I know for sure that George *was* a giant.

George Wilson was a giant of a man.

Even without a few drinks inside of me, at over 6'3" and probably 250 pounds, when he was introduced to me I know there was a part of me that was cowering.

Years later I found out the heart in this man, the caring that he possessed within him, was far larger than any physical presence he emanated. It was a heart that was too big for his body. Unfortunately, literally.

I can still see him in a dark suit with a white shirt and even without knowing him I could tell it wasn't his outfit of choice. Truth was I had no idea where he managed to get such a tailored suit in Asheville. I am not a fashion maven, but it had to have cost him a hundred bucks. I'd say I don't know why I remember this detail, but it would be a lie. I know very well why I remember it.

He was definitely a good looking guy, in *polite* circles the looks of a lady's man, with blonde hair, a square face, and a good nature even in his hand shake that seemed to defy his size. Looking up at him (like I had a choice) I was pulled into his gray/green eyes not knowing that when he got angry they carried the menace of snake eyes.

It was the strongest first impression I ever had or would have of a man in my life. I just didn't know it.

We didn't talk a lot that night; the ladies were far more exciting to both of us than conversation. It never occurred to me nor in any way was I expecting to hear from him again.

A week later he stopped by my house, somewhere between the fourth and fifth bourbon I had given him my address, and over the next five years a friendship grew between us. I guess you could best describe it as a social relationship that grew to a casual friendship to a meaningful friendship.

By 1965 it was a tight friendship bordering on an unexplainable bond.

In 1967 that bond was cast in stone when I began to know the truth behind George Wilson and, more importantly, the truth within him.

It would not be the truly awe inspiring, life threatening, world changing events in his life—and *that* they indeed were, that astonished me.

As horrific as the words would sound as they came from

a man standing only feet away from me, it would not be his connection to *Murder Incorporated* that left me paralyzed.

As earth shattering as the truth was, it was not the revelation of Japan's atomic bomb effort during World War II and his mission—a mission where he was the sole survivor to thwart it, which left me speechless.

It was, and still is, *the man behind the events in his life* that made George Wilson the individual he was.

He was a man who changed my life as he did countless others. He shared his wisdom, the true strength that he possessed, and in so doing made me a different, and better, person.

George, if a cliché was ever more befitting, was David inside of Goliath.

It was not what I learned from him that necessitated this book, it is what he gave to me and with honor I returned.

Friendship.

Men are afraid to use the word love.

I'm not.

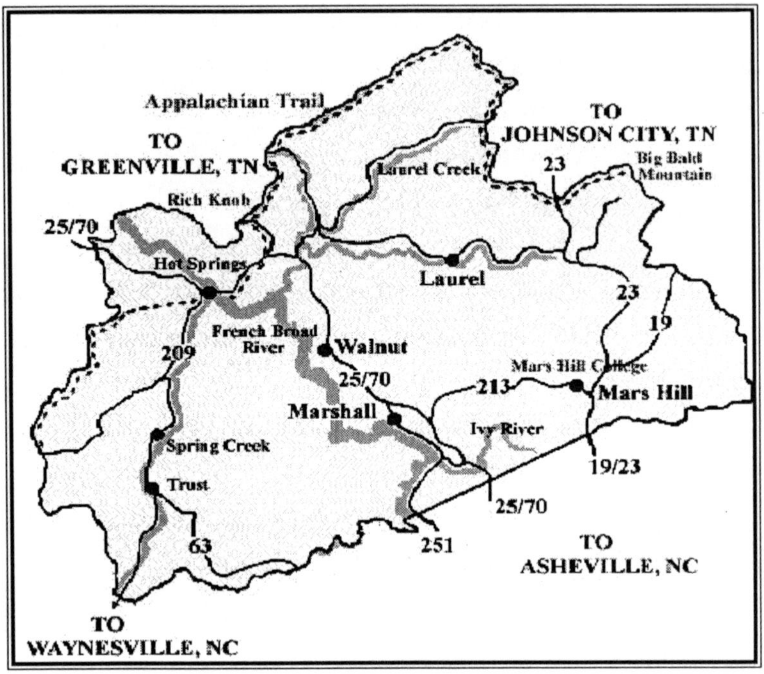
Appalachian Trail
TO
GREENVILLE, TN
TO
JOHNSON CITY, TN
Laurel Creek
23
Big Bald
Mountain
Rich Knob
25/70
Hot Springs
Laurel
23
19
French Broad
River
Walnut
209
25/70
Mars Hill College
213
Mars Hill
Marshall
Ivy River
Spring Creek
19/23
Trust
25/70
63
251
TO
ASHEVILLE, NC
TO
WAYNESVILLE, NC

Chapter One

"Teaching kids to count is fine,
But teaching them what counts is best."
~Bob Talbert~

Today, Marshall, Madison County, North Carolina is considered a rich crossroads of rural Appalachian History, with the French Broad River at its feet, the steep rocky edge of a mountain at its back, a railroad passing through, and a pillared court house. Marshall is, to many, the epitome of a picturesque mountain town.

It is a town proud of its history with the Buncombe County Turnpike passing through, as the location of notorious Civil War events, and as the hub of Madison County commerce for many years. The old-time store, art galleries, and unique gift boutiques lead to a community where folks still say, "hi," on the street as they pass their neighbors. As in the decades preceding, Marshall services the mountain community not only with commerce but with a dedication to neighbors in need. Neighbors who, unlike many places in the country, know the people they pass on the street – by name.

In most cases they think they know all about the person they see at the market, gas station, or town hall meeting. In some cases they are wrong.

In 1921 George Wilson was born in Marshall to a town that would feel the effects of the depression that staggered rural communities across the nation and they would remember George Wilson. The George Wilson they knew, or thought they did.

The Wilsons were "average dirt farmers" in a poor farming community with a couple of cattle, a horse or two, and dogs and chickens roaming their property. They grew corn and vegetables on their land which, along with livestock, were not a means of enterprise but of nourishment.

George had two brothers and one sister all raised by loving parents in what can only be described as a tight knit, caring family. They were a family who were not dictated to by the times they were living in, but by the very foundation of family. Family meant responsibility, and responsibility meant dedication from his parents to "bringing up their children right in a world that forgets the difference between right and wrong and the meanings of morals and values."

His mother, although as kind hearted and maternal as a mother could be, was said to rule with an "iron hand." Her small, petite stature provided a façade for eyes that with one look were said to kill if you strayed from the wrong path. A trait whose power would be passed to her son. In certain circumstances, "wrong path" is relative.

All in all, a philosophy, an ethos, that has seemed to be forgotten as time goes by.

While at an early age George, like most children, struggled with his mother's rules, it wasn't till much later in life that he realized how the simple values of honesty, commitment, loyalty, and caring were ingrained within him. He never needed to learn them. They were there since day one and remained a part of him throughout his life regardless of his circumstances; that word again.

If you asked George about something he remembered most from childhood he would talk about a tornado, the kind of twister that most can only imagine from films, that was coming toward his house on a sky blue day that had him carrying his sister into a shelter only to come out later and see the entire back porch of their house gone. It wasn't a movie.

When you asked him why, he got a small smile on his face as if it was not the tornado that affected him but the clear sky preceding it and the strange, isolated damage after it. He probably never even thought of how he had most likely saved his little sister's life, or how that statement—witnessing absolute calm and utter destruction, materialized throughout his life.

George.

If the question was asked again, this time about a time later in his youth, that memory would be replaced…without the small smile.

In a time when children were often forced out of

necessity to work, at an age when the cost of food shouldn't be on their minds, George's mother refused to have him succumb to the pressures of survival (a "parent's job") and insisted he stay in school. She, like many mothers—or those with her determination and resolve, wanted what was absolutely best for her son and knew that the best, the future, came with education. This was not a choice that the "iron fist" left up for discussion.

George didn't have to struggle in school and, although he probably never admitted it, understood the value of an education.

Education aside, he was a teenager. In George's case that meant two things with them being directly related. The first was sports. With George surpassing six feet by the time he was sixteen, and with a body to match a rhino, he was on the football team. Few opponents relished the day they would see George's eyes piercing through them only feet away. The few that welcomed the challenge regretted it. It was not just his size and strength that empowered George, but the determination behind them. Combined, he became the very definition of a Tackle—blocking, physically keeping defenders away from the offensive player.

Foreshadowing?

Off the field things weren't much different. Without thought George would stick up for anyone who was being pushed around. Then again, just being in the same room with George frightened people off from pushing anyone around.

In essence, his position on the field and the way he was treated and seen by others became his station in life. It would be a life, unbeknownst to him, where if his size wasn't used as a deterrent, his strength was used for the defense and the protection of not only himself, but any good person he was able to assist.

As for point two on being a teenage boy, George was the source behind the theory of the good looking jock getting all the girls. He wasn't ashamed to admit it, he wanted them all. An education he took seriously and ended up earning a doctorate in, for after high school he stopped playing football but he never stopped getting all the girls.

His fun with Suzy, Mary, or Sandy came to an end when at sixteen he was approached by the high school's music teacher who had seen him having sex with a young co-ed.

This was the 1930's.

While it would be hard to visualize this six foot, 220 pound "stud" trembling, that was how he felt when the stereotypical looking, young music teacher confronted him. His trembles turned to confusion, and then to the cockiness that only a sixteen year old lothario could comprehend, when the teacher didn't lecture or threaten him with expulsion or, worse yet, the horror of informing his parents, but became the first of many women to seduce *him*. One would think that the seduction that led to sex between a sixteen year old kid and a teacher would be the first story he remembered from his youth, a story that would bring a much larger grin to his face than that of a tornado.

In this case, he had to outrun the tornado *after* it had hit him.

What George, or any other young man –or woman for that matter– was not prepared for, couldn't even imagine, never contemplated, was that the teacher became pregnant.

Pregnant.

The horror was not his alone as the truth of the situation devastated his mother, quite possibly even more so.

This was the 1930's. Men married pregnant women.

George's mother cared about her son far too much to have his life become determined (ruined?) at such a young age. The morals and principles that were so dear to her were countered by the love for her son. She absolutely could not let her young boy become a married man at the age of sixteen.

In 1937 George was sent to live with relatives in Philadelphia.

He played football there. He got his diploma as his mother always wanted him to there. He "met" a lot of girls there.

When he graduated in 1939 George's life changed.

Dramatically.

That pregnancy did give birth to a new person; only the person was George himself as he entered a life as far away, as vastly contradictory, to the life of Mrs. Wilson's son.

Chapter Two

"Man is made by his belief.
As he believes, so he is."
~Johann Wolfgang von Goethe~

Moving from a rural community, where you knew your neighbors' names and everyone looked out for each other, to the big city, where remembering the names of streets comes before remembering the names of the people on either side of you, can be like waking up on a different planet.

A planet where rules and morals seem to change to suit the city in which you live, rather than the values you were taught to believe. There are approximately 610 miles between Marshall, North Carolina and Philadelphia, Pennsylvania. It could have been measured in light years.

Transferring high schools gave George the chance to keep some semblance of order in a life that could have been the inspiration for *City Mouse – Country Mouse*, as he faced new challenges on the football field with opponents who would soon learn of his fierceness and new conquests in a city that posed a chance of sating George's appetite in the opposite sex.

Philadelphia was a city that enthralled and amazed the teenager who was now reaching 6'3" and 240 pounds from North Carolina and, at times, frightened the boy within who was not just seeing a new kind of life, but a new breed of humanity.

The rural community of his youth faced the depression. The city rebelled against it.

In a time when inflation, anger, uncertainness, and crime were on an unprecedented rise, Philadelphia was a battleground for individual survival while the home he had left behind was a united front against the times rather than each other.

Within months of arrival George had learned a lesson or, more appropriately, taught himself the lesson which

would take him through life; the power to adapt and adjust to his surroundings before they had the chance to conquer him. Within the comfort of his aunt's home, the familiarity of the football field, and of course the new batch of girls to choose from, George began the stage of adapting while adjusting would not be far behind.

After high school there was not a farm for him to return to or a job, even one without any prospects, that was readily available for an eighteen year old kid. Maybe being eighteen and with nothing to compare the state of the economy (or life) to was what made it all seem better, if not easier, for him than others in 1939. Yet, as it was later to become a stigma of his life, he was not one to sit idle waiting for an opportunity to come by. An eighteen year old declares he wants to be on his own, he's a man; his aunt wasn't all that upset that she was getting her house back.

George walked the streets until he came across a bar, an average working man's place that was looking to hire a bartender. He never thought about the *average patrons* that drank at a bar such as this. If he had, he would have wondered why (or how) there was an air of tameness to the place rather than rowdiness. With his size (and a deep baritone voice) the owner never questioned his age and hired him on the spot.

Bartending was a perfect fit for George. He had a special demeanor about him that put people at ease regardless of his size, let them feel wanted in the place, and he had a way of listening to—not just hearing, people when they talked.

The second clue to the establishment should have come to George when that "point three of the population" who didn't steer away from him because of his size but liked to test it, didn't exist in this bar.

A customer could come in one time and from then on he not only remembered what they drank, but what half pint they wanted to take with them. In a working man's bar in 1939, where many customers weren't actually working, he was, to put it simply, friendly. Or, to be more precise, the reflection of friendly that each individual wanted to see.

The "girls" had turned into women and they were just as happy as the rest of the crowd to see George pouring their drinks or *accidentally* touching fingers when money was exchanged. In other words, George had all the gifts a bartender needed to have—and the benefits that go with it.

For the owner, there was that one special gift that George possessed. His size. He wasn't a bouncer, he wasn't an enforcer of rules; he was just the big guy behind the bar that if he couldn't turn everyone friendly he would at least intimidate them. Or was it that the bar itself intimidated them?

Soon, George would learn what actually was behind the bar's intimidation. Soon, the owner would find another use for George besides twisting off a cap or pulling a draft.

Soon, George would be introduced to *Murder (Inc.) Incorporated.*

On November 12, 1941, feared Murder, Inc. hitman-turned-informant Abe "Kid Twist" Reles was found dead from a fall from a hotel window. The evidence suggested that Reles had been pushed, earning him the epithet "The canary who sang, but couldn't fly." The story of the organization that carried out Mob assassinations.

The name was *not* thought up on Fifth Avenue. It was what it portends to be.

Philadelphia, like every major city in the country, succumbed to the true evil, vicious, result of depression. People often hear about men on the street trying to sell apples, children begging for change, or entire families wandering from one avenue to the next in hope of finding something that no longer exists. A city was a place where what jobs that were available were taken for low wages with the hope that unions would "one day" make a difference. For the mean time, it was food on the table. With cities crumbling under the harshness of depression crime rose at levels that had not been seen before in the country. As crime escalated, a new *industry* was born that was not feeling the effects of the depression, but prospering from it.

The *industry* of organized crime along with the innate fear of that one word: Mafia. It was a tight run business that took full advantage of all that had been lost, and wrapped its tentacles around every working man it could. As their influence rose to include all levels of economic, political, and social status, crime became a foundation rather than an exception of growth. Like most businesses, organizations sometimes face dissention and "companies"

dispute over territories and market share. The only difference with the business of *Organized Crime* was how they settled, or *finalized*, their differences.

After the formation of the commission of the National Crime Syndicate, *Murder Incorporated* (*Inc.*) was created as the "enforcement arm" of the Italian and Jewish Mafia.

Though its members (including Louis "Lepke" Buchalter, Albert Anastasia, Lucky Luciano, Meyer Lansky, Dutch Schultz, Benjamin "Bugsy" Siegel, Frank Costello, Harry Pittsburgh Phi" Strauss and Joe Adonis, had assembled into a panel of sorts—sometimes called "The Syndicate" or "Combination") were involved in a variety of illicit activities including loan sharking, prostitution, gambling, bootlegging, and labor racketeering they became infamous for their role in the so called Execution Squad.

"So called" was far from the truth and Execution Squad was nothing more than a fancy name for a band of ruthless killers from Brooklyn (initially) retained to conduct contract killings for the top echelons of organized crime throughout the United States in the 1930s and 1940s.

It has been said that *Murder Inc.* was responsible for between 400 and 1,000 contract killings (with *many* calling that number very low as victims were not always determined; translate: found) utilizing a wide variety of instruments, including ice picks when a gun didn't seem the appropriate message, to murder their victims.

The ruthless killers were paid a regular salary as retainer as well as an average fee of $1,000 to $5,000 per killing.

Murder Incorporated truly was organized crime. It ran like any other business with day to day activities being conducted out of the some of the most common places from store fronts to the back rooms of candy stores… and bars.

The only difference being hit-men getting calls relayed from bosses to kill somebody, not for another scoop of vanilla.

Killings were meticulously planned prior to "the" phone call with "an employee" being responsible for discovering all of the victim's habits, schedules, and planned locations before a hit was undertaken by the killer.

Their motto was, "We only kill our own," which basically meant, they only kill criminals. A convenient, if treacherous, mission statement to live (or die) by.

George Wilson was not a killer, nor had he ever witnessed a murder. George Wilson was a *Defensive* Tackle on the football field; a *defensive* man in life.

His new coach, the kindly bar owner in a Philadelphia working man's bar who hired a kid out of high school, had in effect recruited George for a new team with a new position.

Being young and naïve, George Wilson never realized he had become part of the intricate web of *Murder Incorporated.*

A new position, a new team, a new rule book…but he was not going to change the person underneath the helmet. Hopefully.

Chapter Three

"Things do not change;
We change."
~Henry David Thoreau~

It didn't take long for George to recognize the bourbon drinkers from the whiskey guys to the ones who for some reason drank gin. The vodka guys were the hardest for him. He didn't know if they had crossed the line from a Bloody Mary to a vodka and soda to a Martini or just skipped to vodka on the rocks. They didn't down shots like the others, but they finished drinks before someone's shot glass hit the bar top. While others took their half pint with them when they left, the vodka guys never left without at least a pint, sometimes a fifth. To the ones who didn't work they thought no one would notice they were drinking rather than working and the ones who worked thought no one could smell the vodka on their breath. They weren't fooling anybody but themselves. But they "occasionally" tipped.

There wasn't a menu of forty seven beers for George to remember and describe the color of, as you drank *Schlitz* or didn't come in. *Michelob* was around for a while during a brewer's strike but even (or especially) in a bar, strike and the alcohol produced from it were not mixed company.

Then there were the one or two *gentlemen* who came in every couple of weeks and ordered scotch. Neat, water on the side. *Gentlemen* because they wore suits, not because of the scotch no matter what their intention was. In truth, the suits didn't help them look like gentlemen to anyone but themselves. They weren't the talkative types, hell, they barely ever smiled. After the third time George put out his hand and got air in return he gave up.

These thin, wiry *gentlemen* with out of place polished shoes, creases in their slacks, nonexistent smiles on lips that didn't part, and soulless eyes created a fear—a respect in their warped minds, that intimidated the bar far more than the 250 pounds behind the counter.

He wasn't naïve and, if there had been any innocence in him left over from high school, it vanished hours after he began working at the bar. More precisely, moments after the first refused handshake. Immediately he knew that this place, like any place that sold liquor, did *business*—had a connection with or to, the mob.

He overheard bits of conversations between his boss and people in the back room, always took notice of people with overcoats or an elevated hip when they walked, but kept his nose clean. By now George knew the city, knew what the *elevated* hip meant. If his boss was paying the right guys the right kind of money he figured it was all part of the game.

George didn't know how wrong he was, how high up the totem pole his boss in fact was.

Within weeks of gaining his boss's trust, he was asked to pass an envelope to "one of the scotch drinkers" when they came in. He thought nothing of it. It was the smart thing to do. It became a regular occurrence. Just as regular as the guys not finishing their scotch neat, water on the side and giving him a large tip.

Was he innocent or was it innocence?

How quickly George was told (or found out) of the contents of the envelope is not clear but the information proved just how high up his boss was within the *organization.*

The envelope contained all of the details about an intended victim of *Murder Inc.* The person that the killer, the *scotch drinker*, was hired to eliminate, usually through the choice of his own but exceptions were made given special individuals and their crimes against the *organization.* The envelope with its detailed background of targets, schedules, places of return visits, even addresses of girlfriends that no one was supposed to know about, was the efficient killing dossier that was George's responsibility to pass along for *Murder Incorporated.*

The envelope that passed through his hands is what allowed for the efficient kill to take place. He made it possible.

George's hands were never bloodied, but he knew who he worked for, how he held the death warrants in his hands. He was an official emissary of *Murder Incorporated.* They knew it. He knew it.

ANASTASIA SLAIN IN A HOTEL HERE; LED MURDER, INC.

TWO FIRE 10 SHOTS

Masked Killers Escape —11 Witness Attack in Barber Shop

He was nineteen. He didn't think his hands ever trembled, but he knew there was a gun to his back each time an envelope was in his hand.

He knew the gun would be in front of him if he ever talked. He didn't. He wouldn't. He escalated.

In 1941 George's boss *promoted* him to the gambling side of the business. It was his responsibility to go through town collecting (using the term loosely) money from all of the numbers outfits that his boss ran. It's not sure if it was his size, unveiled threats, the threat of who he worked for, or the combination of all three but George was quite adept at collecting the money owed to the man who was no longer just "the kind guy who gave a kid a job." With George's *efficiency* his boss was able to grow his business throughout the city.

George didn't drink scotch.

In this "circle of business" growth and competition were frowned upon to say the least. On many occasions George was confronted and threatened in order to *set an example* for his boss of what will happen if the growth continued into "territories that weren't his." Threats within the Mafia did *not* involve keying your car or breaking a finger. The horse's head was real. He knew.

While the intimidation was never far from George's mind, it was not until he was cornered by two guys as he was coming out of a weekly money pick up that reality slapped him in the face. George was a large man…but not in-between them, or rather what they were holding. It wasn't that they were blocking his path. A gun was. They forced him into a car and began the *drive*.

With the car speeding and the gun inches from his face he was told to open the door and jump. What was on the exterior was irrelevant. On the inside, George's entire body was in a cold sweat feeling the panic that only those who have had a gun so close to their face that they couldn't see it could fathom.

Whether it was his physical size, mental fortitude, adrenaline, or stupidity, is inconsequential; instead of opening the door his mouth formed the word "No" before his brain knew what it was saying— or maybe his brain knew all along.

Just then they hit a large bump in the road. George, whose panic kicked in with that rush of adrenaline, fear, or maybe just a plain fucked up survival instinct, used his size to his advantage and grabbed the gun away before his abductor realized what was happening. With the gun arcing back and forth between the two guys, unbelievably not shaking while his body trembled beyond the Richter scale and his heart was moments from hearing the word *clear*, he told them that they had the wrong man.

For his assailants it might have been pure fear or it could have been the truth, but the two of them "*let*" George go, which is an interesting concept on their part considering he was three times their size and he was the one with gun.

The Mafia is a strong supporter of the Church. At that moment he knew why.

They had been half right in their assumption; an example had been set for George, if not his boss. Second(s) to death can do that.

With the sweat pouring off of him and his clothes plastered to his still shaking body he returned to his apartment less than an hour later only to be hit with another shock as to the life he was living. His roommate, a refrigerator of a guy, made his living by robbing poker games. Literally. The guy would join a game just for the purpose of stealing—not cheating—money from the players at the table...because gamblers in back rooms were good, safe people to rob?

He knew the guy had gotten into some terrible trouble a night ago stealing money from people who would *not* let his actions go unpaid for, but didn't know how bad it was until he stared into his apartment—empty of everything except garbage, his closet void of all clothing, and a dresser that had dust stains from where his watch had been, were all the result of his stupid, fat, mother—you get the rest—roommate.

In that instant George knew that his life was over if he didn't make a change. It wasn't fits of crying, cursing, or self realization. He had to escape from the life he was living. Or created.

Murder Incorporated surpassed being a killing machine but a plague to all who breathed in its air.

In 1941 the world was on edge, unsure of the future, but knowing that change was coming. So was George.

Chapter Four

"The first and greatest victory is to conquer yourself;
To be conquered by yourself
Is of all things most shameful and vile."
~Plato~

His previous line of work was not something that could be written, or even massaged, on a resume, so George was left to pounding the streets the way millions of Americans were still doing in 1941. However, the shackles of the depression were quickly lifting as America found itself while not active, economically stimulated by the war that had broken out across Europe.

It wouldn't be long before that economic stimulus would enter every phase of industry in America forging the country not only out of depression but into immediate growth.

As such, George didn't have to pound the streets for very long before he found himself working in what would become the booming coal industry; the foundation of steel. Unfortunately, at six foot three and 250 pounds, should George have stayed in the mines any longer than a couple of weeks he would have been driven mad by claustrophobia, killed a co-worker for some extra leg room, or would have been responsible for a cave-in, died, and been discovered as a pre-historic human who walked with his knuckles to the ground.

Shortly after the attack on Pearl Harbor the nation entered into an economic surge far greater than what could be described as growth when the nation found itself at war. The first American businesses to see this drastic infuse of capital were industries that worked with the defense department.

With the war being so far from its shores, America was in need of finding ways in which a greater amount of planes could be transported by freighter (air craft carrier) for the wars in both Europe and the Pacific than the

current use (or waste) of space as destined by wing span. Thus, came the emergence of "folded wing" aircraft that enabled the navy to closely align the vast amount of planes effectively tripling the quantity of cargo transported; cargo—aircraft, utilized to assault our attackers and defend America on two fronts.

George, who had began his adroitness with tools out of necessity on a farm in North Carolina, got a job working the night shift at a company dedicated to not merely maintaining these aircraft but alleviating complications that had arisen through their own innovation. His mechanical skills proved how an "apprentice can go to a master" late one evening when he and his co-worker managed to fix a key element that was not locking the wings into place as it should.

They had solved a problem that truly could have been life threatening shortly before the day's sun had arisen—likely before their manger had pulled back his bedcovers, and made the decision to conceal all knowledge of how the failure was remedied before showing the result to "the man in charge." It was not their intention that the answer to the malfunction was to remain hidden, just properly accredited.

In 1942 George, along with every other patriotic American, joined the war effort actively enlisting in the Navy. When the manager who he had worked for heard of George's enlistment he requested that George tell the Defense Department about the "company's" revolutionary design innovation and went as far as to tell George that he would get a $500 "bonus" for his *assistance.*

George *did* pass along the information to the proper authorities, but *not* for the bonus, but for the chance to help save the lives of his countrymen.

Wanting to be of as much service as possible to his country in an environment where his skills would be required, George was inducted into the *Seabees.*

Seabees are members of the United States Navy construction battalions whose name derives from the initials of Construction and Battalion, hence "cb" pronounced "Seabee(s)"

More than 325,000 men served with the *Seabees* in World War II, fighting and building on six continents and more than 300 islands. In the Pacific, where most of the construction work was needed, the *Seabees* landed soon after the Marines and built major airstrips, bridges, roads, gasoline storage tanks, and Quonset huts for warehouses, hospitals, and housing. They often operated under fire and frequently were forced to take part in the fighting to defend themselves and their construction projects.

It should be noted that the *Seabees* would quote the aforementioned statement as "the Marines landed soon *after* the *Seabees*."

On March 5, all Construction Battalion personnel were officially named *Seabees* by the Navy Department. Admiral Moreell personally furnished them with their motto "*We*

Build, We Fight." A logo, the *Fighting Bee*, was drawn by Walt Disney himself.

In the spring of 1942 George Wilson of Marshall, North Carolina by way of Philadelphia, Pennsylvania, arrived for basic training in San Diego, California on his way to becoming a *Seabee* in the United States Navy.

People say, "History repeats itself." They are wrong. Man repeats history. People say, "They've left their past behind them." Fair enough, but what if the past won't leave you?

George knew his past wouldn't be behind him. It would always be a step ahead of him even if it was lurking in the shadows. Distance meant nothing to people with a phone… and a cousin, nephew, or uncle who were loyal to the *family*.

From the first day of basic training George immediately felt that someone was following him, shadowing his movements. To George this wasn't a psychic sense, but a learned trade. The guy who was hunting—ready as if to pounce upon his prey, was, as strange as it sounds, a man who almost made George look small. The fears, what some might consider paranoia, were in his case the reaction to survival. He knew with certainty that he was not being shadowed out of mere curiosity, but being put on alert (albeit more than likely he wasn't supposed to be aware of his pursuer) by a "representative" from Philadelphia. When the shadowing progressed into bullying and constant taunting he was sure he was being marked.

He was waiting for the moment he was sure to come, only not sure exactly what that moment would entail.

It was the middle of night. At one moment the guy was sitting on his bed. In the time it took George to blink, he was being head butted with the ferocity of a SWAT team pounding a battering ram into a steel door. As the battering ram hit its mark *it* (at the moment the man was not a "he" but a possessed "it") attacked, throwing fists that seemed to land every time they were thrown.

Blood was flowing through George's broken nose as his body inured pounding after pounding to his kidneys, ribs, and skull. He then got in his fair share of abuse as his fist cracked the guy's jaw only adding more blood to the floor of the barracks that would in no way pass inspection in the morning. That is of course if there was any barracks left as they thrashed into beds, tables, and chairs creating the death match for any brave enough to watch two pit bulls fighting for life with jaws and fists clenched. There wasn't a man in the barracks, or compound for that matter, who came within ten feet of the two, not for fear of being hit by blood splatter, but for fear of *their* own blood getting splattered.

At one point George managed to kick the guy between the legs and, while the guy doubled over gasping for air, he went after his attacker only to then be somehow caught in a choke hold. No thoughts ran through his head as to why he was in this fight, or who the man was, but only how to survive. One of those rare times when George was more afraid for himself than what he might do to another person. At that moment, and for many years to come, he would remember the night when he didn't care what he did to stop—to kill, the rabid image in front of him who wanted him dead.

To understand the feeling you would have to experience it, but the fear of a man's body—his eyes, his hands, seeking death is far more horrifying, far more realistic, far more personal as it seeks your life than a piece of steel with its unknown bullets.

There was no question in his mind. "*It was either him or me.*" And the fight continued.

The fight was eventually broken up before one of them got mauled to a pulp without him fully knowing how many people it took to get them apart. Or, who would have remained standing. Or, alive.

With adrenaline pumping though him, blood pumping out of him, and his fists clenched in front of him George knew that even the Navy wasn't going to provide a barrier between him and his past. They wouldn't allow it, and if they knew which barracks he was in today then they could find out when and where he was....anytime.

Ironically, the guy had nothing to do with his past or even with George for that matter, other than the fact that George was the closest in size to the man who was going to be the only top dog in the entire unit. That in itself was reason enough to stalk and attack another human being.

The guy wanted to be "King of the Hill." It was worse than the back streets of Philadelphia, yet wasn't the premise the same?

While the fight would never leave his mind, it was far from the most memorable event during his training in San Diego. Not just for him, but for two – *three* – other people.

He had become close friends with a married couple, one a fellow sailor waiting to ship out, who were desperately trying to have a child. With the war and thousands of miles about to separate them they had found out that it would be impossible for the man to father a child, a link to bind them together.

At their request George agreed to impregnate the woman. While he would never say it so bluntly, as if his contribution to their love was an afterthought, he was providing them with the bond for the man's return. He was not the father, only the sperm, his friend would be the father, his wife the mother. They had their link. To him, he couldn't understand how anyone could refuse their request…a request for champagne rather than scotch.

He wouldn't call it a heartfelt, unselfish act. Most would.

One week later George was aboard a ship heading for Honolulu. There was no way of him knowing what was awaiting him. Or, for that matter, what was awaiting the world.

More importantly, the things the world would never find out about.

Chapter Five

"Courage is resistance to fear, mastery of fear,
Not absence of fear."
~Mark Twain~

Before the skyline of Coronado or the tear filled eyes of loved ones faded from view, the side rails of the ship were bending from the weight of newbie sailors feeding the fish below with whatever was left in their stomachs. Some would get over it quickly. Others would only replace the nausea with the bile that would rise within them a few thousand miles from where they were now standing, or rocking or, in many cases, reciting prayers that would be meaningless compared to those they would cry out in a foxhole.

Hundreds or thousands of pimply faced kids, kids who had gone straight from school dances and mowing the lawn—not a life facing guns and the men behind them on the streets of Philadelphia, now faced a challenge where with a uniform and a salute they were considered men.

These "men" who thought that defying authority might get them detention or a night without dad's car, "men" who barely understood the concept of respect as something more than occasional complacency, were now in the military. The respect, obedience, and dedication to a unit as opposed to the individual that was a necessary requirement in the armed forces was as foreign to them as the lands they were traveling to.

They were not any less dedicated than someone like George who had a clear understanding of the concept of authority (that doesn't mean he liked it, just understood the rules) but they were literally civilians in white and blue – yes, "men" – who with a few weeks of basic training were thought to be, needed to be, soldiers.

It was not that they wouldn't become part of a tight knit military unit that created just as many heroes as casualties, but, on the ship with George heading from San Diego to Honolulu for their first assignments (as only high school kids could define them), their attitudes toward superiors of any level was one of non-compliance. An attitude that can be compared to that of a student and teacher where the student is waiting for a bell to ring while they attempt to keep their eyes open. Compounding their defiance, their new "teachers" were not much, if at all, older than they were.

These sailors who couldn't tolerate the meaning behind the word "sir" were there to kick the shit out of the slant eyed Japs that had bombed their country with as much anger and determination as the people with stripes on their sleeves. It wouldn't take them very long after they landed in their first battle to respect and obey, and, at times, worship their commanders—the men guiding a unit to victory rather than death, who on this three thousand mile voyage across the Pacific were a pain in the ass.

For the moment though, these "young-civilian-soldier-boy-men" thought about the excitement of the battlefield and not the words of a Captain, Lieutenant, or any of the men wearing the stripes that made their voices louder and their backs straighter.

While unlike the "men" on the ship George, who might not necessarily respect but at least acknowledge chain of command, did, as much as he knew he shouldn't and tried to avoid, have a recurring problem with a Chief Petty Officer which lasted for the entire journey. It was not a situation that ever escalated to violence but George knew it would be inevitable if they remained together.

To be in the vastness of the ocean surrounded by men with the same purpose and yet trouble rather the people who embodied it, found George...would there be a place where it wouldn't?

Only days after their arrival in Honolulu the first unit was set to ship out and George "discussed" with the Petty Officer that for both their sakes (a much more congenial word than the word George used or the many going through his head) only one of them should leave the following day; separation being the key to mutual survival.

The Chief Petty Officer, arrogant as ever, insisted that he was the one to go on board, the one who was needed most, while George remained behind.

Many don't believe in fate.

If he was the one who was needed most he was sadly mistaken. The Chief Petty Officer was only days out to sea when the ship was torpedoed and left with no survivors.

George, a fully entrenched *Seabee*, was one of the first to leave the safety of Honolulu days after the Petty Officer's ship had gone down. George's skills in all aspects of construction development from under water welding to mechanical maintenance were needed for the armed forces to invade, capture, and succeed throughout the Pacific Theater.

From the Philippines, Guam, and Wake Island to New Guinea, the Midway, Guadalcanal and places far too numerous to mention in-between, the *Seabees* arrived on shore before the boot prints of Marines were washed away. *Seabees* would vehemently disagree with that order structure.

To these men outside the four walls, walls that the Seabees had constructed, of command headquarters it didn't matter what island they were are on. They were all the same.

Sand, brutal heat, clinging humidity, every sort of insect; Marines, *Seabees*, infantry encountered all these. In addition to the obstacles of the enemy, the troops fought against a variety of terrain and climate where soldiers learned to cope with blistering heat, drenching monsoon rains, and a vicious, rugged world of jungles, volcanoes, and quick sand. They were thrown into one hell hole after another where on the water they faced sharks, barracuda, sea snakes, anemones, razor-sharp coral, polluted waters, and poison fish while on land there was leprosy, typhus, yaws, typhoid, dengue fever, dysentery, saber grass, hordes of flies, snakes and giant lizards.

On one of his first nights serving as a sniper George, atop a bulldozer with a full moon above him, saw something in the water only a few yards from the shore going round in circles. As he lowered himself to get a closer look at the spectacle of frenzied fish, he suddenly felt a wind rush within inches of his head as the sounds of gun shots echoed in his ears.

Many don't believe in fate.

George's first experience with the enemy…and he had inadvertently been saved from death by a school of fish as weeks ago he had inadvertently dodged the enemy's wrath by an obstinate Petty Officer.

It wasn't long after that, or maybe it was—after a few days, *nights* in a jungle on islands that all looked the same time lost meaning, George returned to his tent after a long, what were now fear ridden, late night patrol. There was a rancid smell as he lifted back the tent flaps but with twelve guys sharing a cloth closet and showers a distant memory, he quickly passed out on his cot while the flap of the tent concealed the moonlight and the evils behind it.

Many don't believe in fate.

He was awakened mere minutes, or so he thought, later by and odor that all combat forces recognized; an odor that must have been there when he entered but with the putrid fog of the jungle enveloping him he didn't acknowledge the fumes…or had their bodies not released their bowels while their blood had yet to turn toxic? It was a smell that was inescapable. It was everywhere, and adhered to your clothes, to your body, no matter how many times you washed because you could never wash the pungent smell of death, the instant rotting of a person's insides, from your memory.

He could have been shouting or gaping in horror, but surrounding him all eleven of his bunk mates, twenty-two empty eyes, were staring up at him while blood seeped from their slit throats…a sight that never focused in his hazed, jungle filled eyes minutes ago as he fell into his cot. Which should have been a coffin.

Logic said he had scared the attacker(s) when he entered and when he fell asleep they left without making George number twelve. Truth that doesn't even acknowledge logic said, a missed torpedo, a missed bullet, a missed knife to the throat, how much longer?

The twenty-two lifeless eyes, the eleven speechless throats lined with a blood that to him would never dry, entered his book of never to be forgotten nightmares.

It was going to be a long book.

Chapter Six

"Strength does not come from physical capacity.
It comes from an indomitable will."
~Mahatma Gandhi~

Some individuals wake up in sweat drenched clothes struggling to breathe as a nightmare that has plagued them since childhood once again invades their sleep. In moments calm is returned as they realize the ogre, wolf, or alien that has chased them in their sleep since they were six or seven was nothing but a dream.

Then there are a few that have it far worse. They are the ones that are afraid for their eyes to close knowing that on any given night monsters will invade their sleep leaving them paralyzed beyond a state of fear. They are the monsters that not only steal the peace from your slumber but make you pray that you will not fall back asleep to be awakened by them. It doesn't matter to whom you pray. They'll always be there. They are the nightmares that are real. They never leave.

It is hard to believe that with all George had experienced in such a short life there was one memory, one horror, which remained so vivid in his mind that a nightmare would have been welcomed compared to the reality that he knew; the reality he had seen that he couldn't fathom being created in a man's subconscious let alone in their reality. It was a reality so horrific that made nightmares a blessing.

Even in the light of day, whether alone or trying to share an experience that could not be justly verbalized, the images brought the same trembling terror that had overtaken him that single night in Manila.

It was yet another island in the South Pacific for George until that night. He had seen a lot of death on his tour of duty. This night was a surrealistic experience of fear. A realistic experience of hate. A realistic experience of death as it could never, or should ever, be imagined.

A fear, a bloodshed, brought by Americans to Americans.

On a rare night off he was out with a buddy hitting whatever bar that seemed the closest. In Manila, choice didn't matter as they virtually all had the same whores, water downed drinks, and exhausted boisterous crowds on any evening when soldiers had the *privilege* of trying to erase even a single day's scars. Whether it was the practical rationale of a lack of space, or the even more practical rationale of shelter from artillery, the bars in Manila were located in basements. You entered some non-decrepit door on the street, and followed loud music through a cloud of smoke down six or seven stairs with hopes of reaching the bar.

It was a time when frustration within the military had reached new levels. The anger, the hatred, was particularly festering to the point of explosion by Black men.

Black men angry at Whites and all that that *word* entitled those *privileged* men wearing the same colored *uniform* to.

Soldiers who decided to fight their own war by going AWOL.

But the anger didn't stop with going AWOL. The streets became their own battlefields flooded with muggings, ambushes, and *retaliation* of all degrees against White GIs who had robbed "the Black man" of their dignity, or was it rights, or respect? It didn't matter; the vengeful hate toward the White man was the same. The resulting anger and violence was the same.

There is only one thing worse than pure hatred. Hatred infused by a *heavy* use (or is it abuse?) of all forms of opiate, hallucinogenic, addictive narcotics; all substances that were far from unobtainable in Manila.

On this night in a bar with his buddy, George, along with all the other patrons, looked toward the stairs to see four black men descending brandishing knives. It wasn't the knives that turned the bar into a scene of catatonic chaos, but the look in the men's eyes. Through their opaque, glassy yet barbaric stares there was more than hatred. There was a desire for blood.

Men, soldiers, who had grown accustomed to an enemy's look of terror as they wielded guns or knives, were in a state of paralyzed panic as the lead man inched closer thrusting a switchblade with its smooth, sleek blade ferociously searching its prey while he drowned out all noise below him with a banshee yell.

"I'm gonna kill every Mother Fucker in Here!"

He was heading down the steps in what George could only describe as a drug induced floating cloud, a ghostly image pointing his knife directly at each lone heart throughout the room, with an aura surrounding him that would have frightened the devil, if the devil would have been brave enough to be in the room. With each floating step he came closer to the crowd and George's buddy, out of either fear and the desire for escape or courage and the desire to protect, ran through the crowd and up the stairs.

Fifty years from that moment it would be called a "slasher" film only the films would be far tamer than the truth in that bar.

He barely hit the second step before they began slicing him. They wouldn't stop, just over and over again hacking away at him, filleting him while blood covered anyone within ten feet. He didn't know if his friend was screaming in agony or it was himself crying out in anger as this nightmare kept getting less real, more apocalyptic, within him.

If only the walls were brown. They were white.

The banshee yells, which now had fervor of delight mixed with hate, seemed to drive their possessed bodies closer to the crowd as they built in intensity.

George wasn't sure if he reached to his side or if it had

been there all along, but he had his 45, a gun that was *never* far from him, in his hand as he shot at the lead ape coming closer. His movements were as dreamlike as the massacre, as vivid as the once white walls, and as profound as slow motion. The guy didn't stop. One slug from a 45 was supposed to kill someone…or was the guy not human?

George fired again. The man didn't stop. Was the guy immune to pain in his drug induced stupor? And again he shot with the weapon that was supposed to bring a man down with one bullet. The guy who thought he was immortal, or who was dead and didn't know it anymore than a bear shot in the head whose body keeps on propelling, finally went down. It could have been seconds, if seconds lasted an eternity.

Without a breath in-between, if he had indeed been breathing since the moment their knives had devoured his friend, he took aim at the other three madmen and never stopped shooting until two more were on the ground while the fourth ran up and out to the street. He would have chased him if his legs would have let him.

George didn't notice their bodies on the floor. He was too much in shock at the sight of the bloodied corpse, what was left of his friend, lying where he had been tossed from the steps amid the butchery.

Hell finally had an indisputable definition.

Very soon this would actually *not* be George's worse nightmare from the war. What was awaiting him would be his own purgatory.

It would be a purgatory that would never let him sleep on a night where the images of death would be far *bloodier within him* than what he could see on the floor of a bar in a basement in Manila.

Chapter Seven

"We are going to have peace even if we have to fight for it."
~Dwight D. Eisenhower~

In war they are not called secrets, but things you do not need to know. In war they are not called attacks, but missions. In war it is not called national security, but national survival. In war…it is called war.

In a war it is still called death.

Days after what he could only think of as the devil manifesting on earth, he could still see the blood of his friend on his hands as he had cradled him laying at the foot of the stairs when the screams of the crowd had stopped while the apparitions that had descended the steps would forever be in his dreams. Yet, he locked (or so he hoped) all thoughts of that vile night into a vault within his mind when he was taken to an airfield where he and seven other soldiers were to be flown to an island that might or might not have existed on a map. As the plane alit on a makeshift runway there was confusion among the eight men who had no idea why they were banded together or where they were going. They had been given orders. The days of questions and insolence were long gone...along with the days of innocence.

Like most soldiers in war they had done what was welcomed on a plane miles above sniper fire. They slept.

They were taken to a barracks removed from any activity where they encountered the pictorial definition of a drill sergeant. When he opened his mouth and the commands started spewing out he actually put drill sergeants to shame. Then began what George could only describe as the most intense physical training he had ever undergone without any explanation as to why he was there or what he was in training for. It was harsh enough to be considered punishment...but for what?

The physical limits of exhaustion were soon tested by instruction in hand-to-hand combat including knives, clubs...anything that could be utilized as a weapon. The intensity of their daily rigor became even more terrifying as the men's proficiency of death was catapulted to include all aspects of explosives.

All this time George was still bewildered as to why he was there. He knew they were being molded for a mission that required techniques that few others were familiar with, let alone *Seabees*, but his questions—spoken and otherwise, were answered with more lessons, more structure, and more intensity that gave the purpose of their efforts a surreal, dire nature. He had no idea how close he was to the truth. Within weeks mental alertness was hammered into them as being as vital as the bombs, knives, and guns they were mastering.

For a time George wondered if he was on this strange island with the sergeant from hell being prepared for a battle that he knew nothing about because of his history. Was it his background in mechanics, his skills with guns, courage, determination…or secrecy and silence? Had they researched his past and thought he was needed for whatever was going to occur…or was he expendable?

The confusion and frustration over whatever it was that they were training for magnified when the lessons switched from violence to becoming masters of a compass as if it was a lifeline. Unbeknownst to George, it was.

As the mission drew nearer, although time and destination not disclosed, their instructions in combat, explosives, and the compass- which no one still understood the necessity of, instilled within them, they began to learn the strategy for their upcoming attack. It was a mission of combat, an insurgence by eight "elite" men, which had an urgency that George had never witnessed.

Each member of the eight team squad was assigned special functions to ensure maximum success of what they now clearly understood as a "mission vital to the outcome of the war." They were told in detail (structural not utilization) about the facility they were ambushing and intricate plans were memorized as to where each of them was to place their explosive that would destroy whatever was being held inside. It was a mission of demolition; a covert one with a magnitude of importance that didn't need to be explained.

To ensure maximum secrecy they were not informed

of their departure until the night before they were to leave. They were going to be flown into enemy territory under the cover of darkness, left to penetrate the jungle, set their explosives in the predestinated perimeters of their target, and detonate the devices to an unsuspecting Japanese enemy (which would outnumber them at least ten to one) that most likely had as much knowledge of the intense potential power of what they were guarding as the eight soldiers did.

In all fairness, few in the world did.

It was then imperative that they race undiscovered to the designated pick up place for immediate departure knowing the Japanese would be out in full force once the explosions started. The Japanese soldiers, which had been assigned to protect something they were as unlikely as the eight on this mission to be privy as to and, more than likely, were ingrained with the same intensity, would retaliate with the same ferociousness that had been the directive of George and his men.

Intensive training, what seemed limitless funds, secrecy beyond anything he had experienced, and worth the lives of eight men…but for what?

Before he had left on the mission George was given strict instructions that after the detonations and amid the melee he was to hide in the jungle just at the outskirts of where the plane was idling for the retrieval of what should have been heroes, and when he saw the seventh man jump aboard he was then to race to the plane. It was his job to be the last man on. Like all in the mission, no explanations.

The Japanese had either figured out where their plane had landed or had followed them, and bullets started flying from what sounded like, and most likely was, hundreds of guns. George, anticipating his run as he saw the seventh man get to the foot of the plane, watched in horror as the soldier's head was blown apart from his body. They kept shooting as all hell broke loose until the plane caught fire and all were annihilated.

In his state of internal hysteria he had no idea if the Japanese knew there was an eighth man nearby. But he knew they would begin searching…not merely for him, but for answers. Escape was not merely primal but imperative as there would be a reward offered for the capture of the man who had destroyed…? He knew they wouldn't give up. He didn't want to imagine what would happen if they captured him

He was alone. In a jungle. With a compass.

He, like the other seven, had been told if for any reason he was not (or could not be) picked up by the plane he would need to escape his pursuers by travelling at night to a rendezvous point at the shore where a submarine would surface each night for thirty days.

Without the compass there is no doubt George Wilson would have died in that jungle…after torture.

Rule one on the very first day of training: *No one could ever learn about him or the mission.* No reason given.

Rule one on the night before they left for their mission: *No one could ever learn about them or the mission.* No reason given.

Rule one he repeated on that night watching his squad die as the Japanese were shouting: *No one could ever learn about him or the mission.* Reason was not an issue. He now knew the value of his target regardless of what it was…yet.

He traveled at night following the compass hoping it was leading him to the sea afraid of every noise, every rustle of leaves. It was after two, three days of night travel and day-time vigil that his sweat covered, filth encrusted, insect ravaged body fell sleeping to the ground.

He awoke to being poked and, with his hand on his gun even before he knew where he was, he opened his eyes to a small Chinese child looking down at him, all innocent and smiling. Being led by the hand George was taken to the child's house where he was greeted by smiling parents who offered him food and water.

Late at night, lying on a mat in their small home, he realized what had to be done. He had no choice, and it was a choice that would haunt him for the rest of his life. It was the purgatory he would never escape.

No one could ever learn about him or the mission. No whispers, no one could be tempted by rewards. No acknowledgment of his presence.

The unspoken rule that surpassed rule number one: "*You Don't Leave Anybody Who Knows Anything Behind.*" No exceptions.

George focused on his compass while he crawled through the jungle as opposed to the images of the three guiltless people who had helped him, most likely rescued him, now lying dead on the floor of their small hut.

His eyes were staring at the arrow pointing north while his mind would *always* be staring at the tiny, red hole in the center of the boy's forehead. He had had no choice.

"You Don't Leave Anybody Who Knew Anything Behind." No exceptions.

At the coast, only fifteen miles from where he had been responsible for a sabotage that possibly, undoubtedly, changed the course of world history—a secret mission intent to save the world as we know it, George rendezvoused with the submarine that would take him away from this place, but not his memories…his questions…his nightmares.

He left the shores of *Manchuria* not knowing he was the lone survivor of eight men who had just demolished the only Japanese *Heavy Water* manufacturing plant.

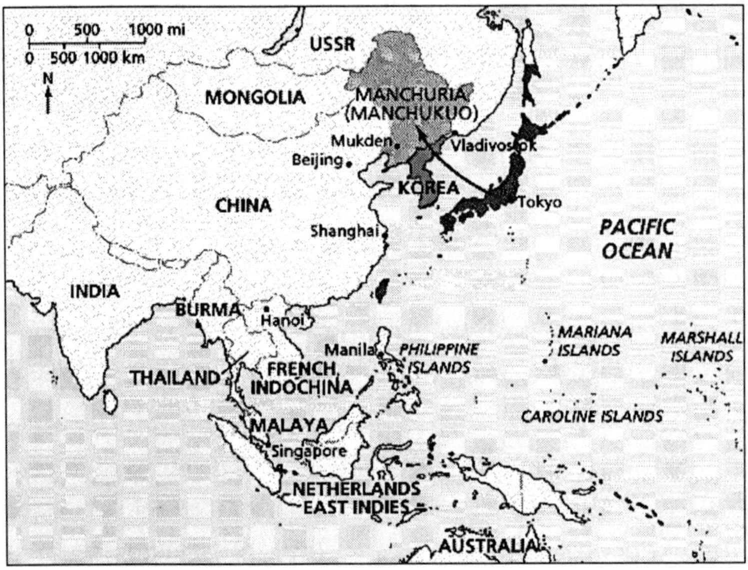

It was not the only time the allies sabotaged a Heavy Water manufacturing plant during World War II.

He didn't know what *Heavy Water* was.

Most people didn't.

He didn't know what an atomic bomb was.

Most people didn't.

No one outside the men responsible for that night's mission ever knew what was in Manchuria and what it could have meant should it have been left standing.

Until now...and how soon after Norway...

Chapter Eight

"We defend and we build a way of life, not for America alone, but for all mankind."
~Franklin D. Roosevelt~

. . . The Norwegian heavy water sabotage was a series of actions undertaken by Norwegian saboteurs during World War II to prevent the German nuclear energy project from acquiring heavy water (deuterium oxide), which could be used to produce nuclear weapons. Physicists everywhere realized that if chain reactions could be tamed, fission could lead to a promising new source of power, albeit the extent and future use it would play in the world was unknown. What was needed was a substance that could "moderate" the energy of neutrons emitted in radioactive decay, so that they could be captured by other fissile nuclei. Heavy water was the prime candidate for moderating the energy of neutrons.

...Heavy water occurs in very low concentrations in normal water but is more concentrated in the residue of water used as an electrolyte. An analysis of the residues from the Norwegian Vemork hydroelectric plant, a large-scale hydrogen production plant using electrolysis of water for ammonia production, showed a far greater concentration.

...Leif Tronstad, then a lecturer at the Norwegian Institute of Technology and Jomar Brun, head of the hydrogen plant put forward a proposal in 1933, the year heavy water was first isolated, for a project, which was accepted by Norsk Hydro and production started in 1935.

...As a result, Norsk Hydro became the heavy water supplier for the world's scientific community.

...Until its sabotage.

...The leading figure in the Japanese atomic program was Dr. Yoshio Nishina, a close associate of Niels Bohr and a contemporary of Albert Einstein.

... In 1939 Nishina recognized the military potential of nuclear fission, and was worried that the Americans were working on a nuclear weapon which might be used against Japan.

...The Japanese fission project did not formally begin until April 1941 at Nishina's Nuclear Research Laboratory which had over 100 researchers.

... The Imperial Japanese Navy's Technology Research Institute had been pursuing its own separate investigations, and had engaged professors from the Imperial University, Tokyo, which then resulted in the formation of the Committee on Research in the Application of Nuclear Physics.

The necessity for heavy water in the production of atomic weapons is a fact.

The Heavy Water manufacturing plant in Manchuria is a fact – not a rumor.

The destruction of the facility was never revealed by the United States but George Wilson was there.

If not for the bravery of eight men on a covert mission in Manchuria, would the Japanese have realized and utilized the power of atomic energy before the United States…

Japan Developed Atom Bomb; Russians Grabbed Scientists

THE ATLANTA CONSTITUTION

Actual Test Was Success

Hull's Condition Is Still Critical

Factory Output Here Now $600,000,000

10 Killed In Crash Of B-29

Baruch Hits Wallace On Atom Views

Copyright 1946 by the Atlanta Constitutional and David Snell.

ACTUAL TEST WAS A SUCCESS

Japan developed and successfully tested an atomic bomb three days prior to the end of the war.

She destroyed unfinished atomic bombs, secret papers and her atomic bomb plans only hours before the

> advance units of the Russian Army moved into Konan, Korea, site of the project.
>
> Japanese scientists who developed the bomb are now in Moscow, prisoners of the Russians. They were tortured by their captors seeking atomic "know-how."

The Konan area is under rigid Russian control. They permit no American to visit the area. Once, even after the war, an American B-29 Superfortress en route to Konan was shot down by four Russian Yak fighters from nearby Hammung Airfield.

I learned this information from a Japanese officer, who said he was in charge of counter intelligence at the Konan project before the fall of Japan. He gave names, dates, facts and figures on the Japanese atomic project, which I submitted to United States Army Intelligence in Seoul. The War Department is withholding much of the information. To protect the man that told me this story, and at the request of the Army, he is here given a pseudonym, Capt. Tsetusuo Wakabayashi.

The story may throw light on Stalin's recent statement that America will not long have a monopoly on atomic weapons. Possibly also helps explains the stand taken by Henry A. Wallace. Perhaps also, it will help explain the heretofore unaccountable stalling of the Japanese in accepting our surrender terms as the Allies agreed to allow Hirohito to continue as puppet emperor. And perhaps it will throw light new light on the shooting down by the Russians of our B-29 on Aug. 29, 1945, in the Konan area.

When told this story, I was an agent with the Twenty-Fourth Criminal Investigation Department, operating in Korea. I was able to interview Capt. Wakabayashi, not as an investigator or as a member of the armed forces, but as a newspaperman. He was advised and understood thoroughly, that he was speaking for publication.

He was in Seoul, en route to Japan as a repatriate. The interview took place in a former Shinto temple on a mount overlooking Korea's capital city. The shrine had been converted into an hotel for transient Japanese en route to their homeland.

Since V-J Day wisps of information have drifted into the hands of U.S. Army Intelligence of the existence of a gigantic and mystery-shrouded industrial project operated during the closing months of the war in a mountain vastness near the Northern Korean coastal city of Konan. It was near here that Japan's uranium supply was said to exist.

This, the most complete account of activities at Konan to reach American ears, is believed to be the first time Japanese silence has been broken on the subject.

In a cave in a mountain near Konan, men worked against time, in final assembly of genzai bakuden, Japan's name for the atomic bomb. It was August 10, 1945 (Japanese time), only four days after an atomic bomb flashed in the sky over Hiroshima, and five days before Japan surrendered.

To the north, Russian hordes were spilling into Manchuria.

Shortly after midnight of that day a convey of Japanese trucks moved from the mouth of the cave, past watchful sentries. The trucks wound through valleys, past sleeping farm villages. It was August, and frogs in the mud of terraced rice paddies sang in a still night. In the cool predawn Japanese scientists and engineers loaded genzai bakudan aboard a ship in Konan.

Off the coast near an inlet in the Sea of Japan more frantic preparations were under way. All that day and night ancient ships, junks and fishing vessels moved into the anchorage.

Before dawn on Aug. 12 a robot launch chugged through the ships at anchor and beached itself on the inlet. Its passenger was genzai bakudan. A clock ticked.

The observers were 20 miles away. This waiting was difficult and strange to men who had worked relentlessly so long who knew their job had been completed too late.

OBSERVORS BLINDED BY FLASH

The light in the east where Japan lay grew brighter. The moment the sun peeped over the sea there was a burst of light at the anchorage blinding the observers who wore welders' glasses. The ball of fire was estimated to be 1,000 yards in diameter. A multicolored cloud of vapors boiled toward the heavens then mushroomed in the stratosphere.

The churn of water and vapor obscured the vessels directly under the burst. Ships and junks on the fringe burned fiercely at anchor. When the atmosphere cleared slightly the observers could detect several vessels had vanished.

Genzai bakudun in that moment had matched the brilliance of the rising sun in the east.

Japan had perfected and successfully tested an atomic bomb as cataclysmic as those that withered Hiroshimo and Nagasaki.

The time was short. The war was roaring to its climax. The advancing Russians would arrive at Konan before the weapon could be mounted in the ready Kamikaze planes to be thrown against any attempted landing by American troops on Japan's shores.

It was a difficult decision. But it had to be made.

The observers sped across the water, back to Konan. With the advance units of the Russian Army only hours away, the final scene of this *gotterdammerung* began. The scientists and engineers smashed machines, and destroyed partially completed genzai bakudans.

Before Russian columns reached Konan, dynamite sealed the secrets of the cave. But the Russians had come so quickly that the scientists could not escape.

This is the story told me by Capt. Wakabayashi.

Japan's struggle to produce and atomic weapon began in 1938, when German and Japanese scientists met to discuss a possible military use of energy locked in the atom.

No technical information was exchanged, only theories.

In 1940 the Nisina Laboratory of the Institute of Physical and Chemical Research in Tokyo had built one of the largest cyclotrons in the world. (Cyclotrons found in Tokyo by the invading Yanks were destroyed).

THOUGHT ATOMIC BOMB RISKY

The scientists continued to study atomic theory during the early days of the war, but it was not until the Unites States began to carry the war to Japan that they were able to interest the Government in a full-scale atomic project. Heretofore, the Government had considered such a venture too risky and too expensive. During the years following Pearl Harbor, Japan's militarists believed the Unites States could be defeated without the use of atomic weapons.

When task forces and invasion spearheads brought the war ever closer to the Japanese mainland, the Japanese Navy undertook the production of the atomic bomb as defense against amphibious operations. Atomic bombs were to be flown against Allied ships in Kamikaze suicide planes.

Capt. Wakabayashi estimated the area of total destruction of the bomb at one square mile.

The project was started at Nagoya, but its removal to Korea was necessitated when the B-29's began to lash industrial cities on the mainland of Japan.

"I consider the B-29 the primary weapon in the defeat of Japan" Capt. Wakabayashi declared. "The B-29 caused our project to be moved to Korea. We lost three months in the transfer. We would have had genzai bakudan three months earlier if it had not been for the B-29."

The Korean project was staffed by about 40,000 Japanese workers, of whom approximately 25,000 were trained engineers and scientists. The organization of the plant was set up so that the workers were restricted to their areas. The inner sanctum of the plant was deep in a cave. Here only 400 specialists worked.

KEPT IN DARK ON EACH OTHER'S WORK

One scientist was master director of the entire project. Six others, all eminent Japanese scientists were in charge of six phases of the bomb's production. Each of these six men were kept in ignorance of the work of the other five. (Names of these scientists are withheld by Army censorship).

The Russian's took most of the trained personnel prisoner, including the seven key men. One of the seven escaped in June, 1946, and fled to the American zone of occupation in Korea. U.S. Army Intelligence interrogated this man. Capt. Wakabayashi talked to him in Seoul. The scientist told of having been tortured by the Russians. He said all seven were tortured.

Capt. Wakabayashi said he learned from this scientist that the other six had been removed to Moscow.

"The Russians thrust burning splinters under the fingertips of these men. They poured water into their nasal passages.

Our Japanese scientists will suffer death before they disclose their secrets to the Russians," he declared.

Capt. Wakabayashi said the Russians are making and extensive study of the Konan region.

When Edwin Pauley of the War Reparations Committee, inspected Northern Korea, he was allowed to see only certain areas, and was kept under rigid Russian supervision.

On Aug. 29, 1945, an American B-29 headed for Konan with a cargo of food and medical supplies, to be dropped over an Allied prisoner of war camp there. Four Russian Yak fighters from nearby Hammung Airfield circled the B-29 and signaled the pilot to land on the Hammung strip.

PILOT REFUSES; REDS FIRE

Lt. Jose H. Queen of Ashland, KY., pilot, refused to do so because the field was small, and headed back toward the Saipon base, to return "when things got straightened out with the Russians." Ten miles off the coast the Yak fighters opened fire and shot the B-29 down. None of the crew of 12 men were injured, although a Russian fighter strafed but missed Radio Operator Douglas Arthur.

The Russian later told Lt. Queen they saw the American markings but "weren't sure." because sometimes the Germans used American markings and they thought the Japs might too. This was nearly two weeks after the war ended.

Capt. Wakabayashi said the Japanese Counter Intelligence Corps at least a year before the atom bombing of Hiroshima learned there was a vast and mysterious project

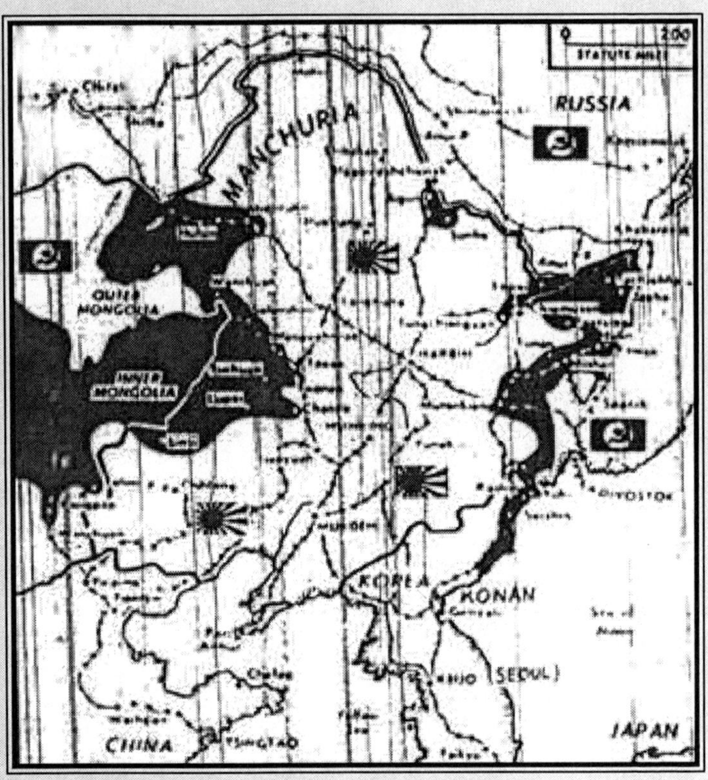

Korea August 1945

When Japs Tested Atom Bomb—This was the war map of Korea in August, 1945, when the Russian spearhead pushed down the western coast in the drive on Konan, site of the Japanese atomic project. The atomic test was made at an unchartered inlet in the Sea of Japan. Today the 38th parallel just above Seoul divides Russian occupied territory from American. Konan remains tightly under Russian control. Russian proximity to Konan prompted the Japs decision to destroy the bomb.

in the mountains of the eastern part of the United States. (Presumably the Manhattan project at Oak Ridge, Tenn). They believed, but were not sure, that atomic weapons were being produced there.

On the hand, he said, Allied Intelligence must have know of the atomic project at Konan, because of the perfect timing of the Hiroshimo bombing only six days before the long-scheduled Japanese naval test.

Perhaps here is the answer to moralists who question the decision of the United States to drop an atomic bomb.

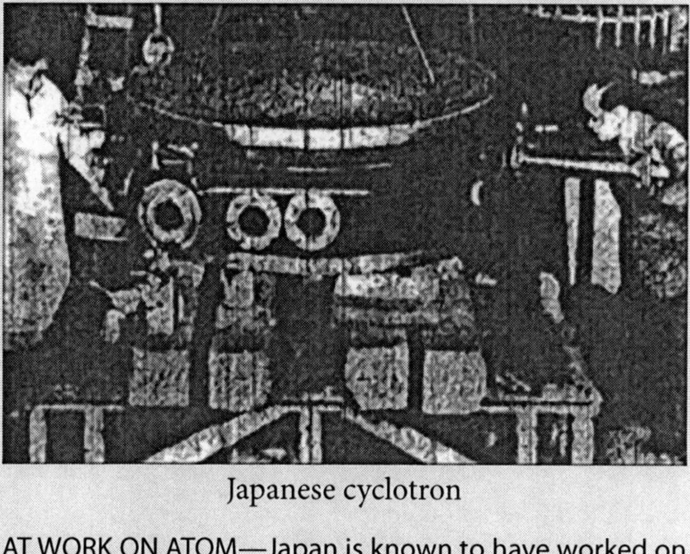

Japanese cyclotron

AT WORK ON ATOM—Japan is known to have worked on Atomic energy as evidenced by this picture printed in 1940 showing an atom-smashing cyclotron. Such equipment was discovered by the U.S. Army after Japan's surrender and was destroyed by the Army then.

The Japanese office, the interpreter and I sipped aromatic green tea as Capt. Wakabayashi unfolded his great and perhaps world-shaking story. His eyes flashed with pride behind the black-rimmed glassed. When the interview ended, he ushered us to the door and bowed very low.

NEWS TO ME GROVES SAYS OF JAPANESE ATOM Bomb.Washington, Oct. 2 (UP).

Major General Leslie Groves, Chief of the atom bomb Manhattan project said Wednesday night when informed of reports that Japan explored a test A-bomb three days before surrender.

"I would be very much interested if the story were true."

"It's all news to me."

War Department officials declined immediate comment on the story carried by the Atlanta Constitution which said that the writer, recently returned from duty with a criminal investigation detachment, had given his information to the American Army Intelligence Unit in Seoul, Korea.

Dr. Carl T. Compton, President of Massachusetts Institute of Technology, told a Senate Committee a year ago that Japan had been trying to develop an A-bomb but that the effort failed for two reasons: Japanese physicists reached mistaken conclusions, B-29 attacks demolished the laboratory where such experiments were being conducted.

American forces entering Japan after the surrender of the nation discovered a cyclotron (an atomic splitting device used by laboratories) and destroyed the instrument.

Many military experts concerned with atomic development contend that Germany was far more advanced than any other nation except the American, British and Canadian teams in the race to produce an A-bomb.

German scientists were known to have made substantial strides in research before the military collapse of the Reich. Indeed it is recorded that non-Nazi scientists who fled Germany contributed valuable knowledge to the research which ended in production of the first A-bomb in New Mexico.

JAPAN SOUGHT PEACE THROUGH RUSSIA NEARLY MONTH BEFORE FIRST A-BOMB.

New York, Oct. 2—-(UP).

America's submarines and pre-atomic bombers had Japan so thoroughly whipped that the Emperor sought peace through neutral Russia nearly a month before Hiroshimo's destruction. Long before that, Japan had periodically tried to make peace with China.

The inside Japan story is told in "The Lost War" published Wednesday by Alfred A. Knopf. The author is Masuo Kato prominent Japanese correspondent for 20 years. Kato was in Washington for Domei News Agency when the war started, and was repatriated. When Domei was dissolved after the war, the American educated Kato became managing editor of the Kyodo News Agency.

Writing in traditional newspaper important things first style, Kato starts his book with this lead paragraph:

The thunderous arrival of the first atomic bomb at Hiroshima was only a coup de grace for an empire already struggling in particularly agonizing death throes. The world's newest and most devastating of weapons had floated out of the summer sky to destroy a city at a stroke, but its arrival had small effect on the outcome of the war between Japan and the United States.

CITES BUNGLING.

Kato assured Allied readers, already aware of their own "bureaucratic bungling" during the war, that the totalitarian Japan's bungling was far worse. He describes incessant Army-Navy-civilian jealousy, the drafting of vital skilled workers for frontline duty, and poor planning in almost all phases of the war effort. Even Cabinet members were kept from knowing Allied progress against Japan.

He records a little bitterly the Japanese Army's absurd effort to hide the truth even when the nation was all but crushed. Because of this he believes no people could hate its leaders more than the Japanese people hated their military by the spring of 1945.

Revealing that Emperor Hirohito finally overruled the military clique that had dominated him throughout the war, Kato relates the surrender developments in these words:

Japan's diplomatic maneuvering for peace dated from the negotiations by Russia in April 1945, that her neutrality agreement with Japan had lost its significance in view of the war between Japan and Russia's allies."

-30-

George would never forget the dot of blood on the boy's forehead or his parents lying by his side. Later he wouldn't forget Hiroshima and Nagasaki. Later he wondered if San Francisco or Los Angeles would have been hit first if heavy water on Manchuria had…

Chapter Nine

"Moral excellence comes about as a result of habit.
We become just by doing just acts,
Temperate by doing temperate acts,
Brave by doing brave acts."
~Aristotle~

It might have been less than seventy-two hours under the sea, but to George it felt like an eternity.

He had been on a secret mission. A mission vital enough that the United States Navy commandeered a submarine to hide in the waters near the coast of Manchuria for thirty nights to rescue him…should he somehow survive. Were they rescuing him or protecting the mission?

His feet dangled off a bed that was not made for someone of George's height as he wondered how a hundred men trapped in a metal tube the size of a Philly cheese steak moved underneath an ocean that had the power to lift vessels high above its crests.

He, along with a team of seven men lying dead somewhere in a jungle, was responsible for destroying a manufacturing plant that was developing a weapon that had the potential ability to surpass anything in the US arsenal. That much had been implied.

What the implication meant was beyond comprehension.

Unlike the crew on board he had never undergone tests to see if his ears could withstand the pressure of being God knows how many miles under the sea nor had he been evaluated for claustrophobia. If it was even possible that a man of his size could not be claustrophobic living in a place where he could barely stand erect without hitting an entanglement of pipes, valves, and levers; all damp leaving one to wonder why.

What in the world was Heavy Water and how it could it be vital enough for seven men to die…vital enough that a child…?

It was said that the air on a submarine circulates constantly providing a flow of clean habitability to a vessel filed with men who, out of constant necessity, adapted to ever changing conditions. He could deal with the rancid stench of a hundred men living in their own sweat. He wondered if the smell of oil ever left your skin.

How come no one, not even the officers of this submarine, were privy to what it was he had done before they rescued him? Or were they?

The days under the ocean passed without sunrises or sunsets as the parts of his body that could lain on a berth that had probably held hundreds of men before him. Time was irrelevant as the pillow brought only one thing to mind… the hole he had put into the boy's head.

From the day training had begun he never doubted for a moment the importance of what he and seven men were being entrusted with, but what in God's name was so earth shattering, so fear evoking, that it necessitated the phrase that would forever haunt him: "You Don't Leave Anybody Who Knows Anything Behind." *No exceptions. And what was Heavy Water?*

The physical confinement of the submarine and the immeasurable pressure being placed upon it by an unforgiving ocean would leave George when the sun returned to his face.

Mentally, the confinement, the pressure, the lack of daylight would always be within him afraid of what each dawn could bring while never doubting what would return in the next night's darkness.

The war in Europe had come to an end when George had been assigned to the South China Sea where he actually welcomed what he had come to consider *normalcy*. In a contradiction to the hate and death that had surrounded him, George met a Chinese girl who was not a one-night stand—a port in the storm, but a girl he grew attached to, a girl he truly cared about. Or, was it a human closeness his brain required if not his heart? Subsequently, could it be as simple as life versus death?

When it was time for him to leave for his next posting the true nature of George rose from its core as he worried about the girl's survival. He didn't have to speculate, he knew she would be shunned by her entire community. A whore, a traitor. That is if she was lucky enough to only be shunned.

War changes a man, but there are some things that aren't changed by bullets, bombs, or torpedoes.

It didn't matter that he was six time zones from home and it didn't matter if the venue was an alley behind the school, the backroom of a bar, or the floor of a barracks in some country whose language had too many vowels. It didn't matter what continent he was on, whether the sounds of guns blaring could be heard over the shouts of men in a circle, or if there was a copper around the corner from a schoolyard, George was a gambler.

He loved the throw of the dice and, as in his life, the potential rewards outshined the possible snake-eyes. The man was addicted to the thrill of the throw, the expectation of winning, and the adrenaline of taking chances. For some, life doesn't imitate art—it imitates reality…be it on your knees or in a jungle.

Only two nights before he was leaving China and *his girl* behind, he had won $1000—US dollars—in a craps game.

He took his entire winnings, converted it into Chinese currency, *filled* a duffle bag (an exchange rate that made a thousand US look like a million), and left it for the girl he wanted to protect long after he was gone. He wanted to be her salvation as she had been for him.

"*You don't leave anyone behind*" can have many different meanings. Some worth remembering, some incapable of forgetting.

As his tour of duty was to come to an end, George was in Japan during the invasion and surrender to a war that had cost thousands, *hundreds* of thousands of lives. While any sort of "peaceful transition" was far from occurring, George met a beautiful Japanese woman. There probably is a Japanese word for déjà vu, but in George's case the "beautiful woman" was no more than a life long recurring theme for him. When she found out he had two sons back in the States *her mission* began. Sons!

She took "this handsome specimen of a man" home to meet her two daughters; daughters who had to have sons! And, a man who would give her daughters' sons would be treated with all she could offer.

While at the woman's home her son returned from the war. He was a son who left as a boy like the acne pocked kids throwing up over the side of a boat but came back as a man, a broken and angry man not only about defeat, but about death, the death caused by Americans. Death to his friends, defeat to his country.

It might have been his home he was returning to, but it was, as it always had been and would be, his mother's house. And in her house, at his mother's table, there was this American, the enemy, the man he had been trained to kill was at his table. The devil's mignon was not merely eating his food, but debasing—mocking—his family while he sat there with that いまいましい American smile on his face and a fork in his face. A smile that days ago he would have been applauded for cutting off.

From the moment the son walked into the house George felt under siege, he felt that the man's eyes were shadowing, calculating his every movement leaving George to wonder when, not if, the daggers in the kid's eyes would turn to daggers in his hand. George was tired of fighting. He was tired of killing. And he was scared—for the son, for the mother, for the daughters...and for himself.

Somehow, as the days went by, the animosity between the two began to lift. It wasn't much, but it felt to George that their two such different cultures were being appreciated, not affiliated, but tolerated by these two men where death had been their only connection.

Before George left Japan that toleration actually grew into a friendship; not a friendship of companionship, but one formed out of respect for an individual rather than the abhorrence of a uniform. Only time would tell what that meant, but it was a beginning, even if only between two men.

He never knew how ironic it was that he, a man set down to sabotage some sort of facility in a place known as Manchuria, and this man—no, this boy, were a single step in a bridge to peace at the end of a catastrophic war.

A war that ended in a land that had been set afire by an atomic bomb.

Heavy Water.

Chapter Ten

"One person's dreams are another person's nightmares.
One person's nightmares are another person's reality."
~Anne Frank~

At the end of the war boys came back as hardened men. They left with innocent eyes to protect the country they loved with nothing but a picture of their girl to pin to whatever wall they could find. They returned after witnessing death in all of its hellish forms to lives they weren't prepared for in hopes that the girl that had been pinned to their locker would be waiting for them.

At ticket tape parades there was more than one soldier who cringed when something fell on his shoulder or a scream from the crowd came at him unprepared.

George returned not having grown from a boy to a man but from a man who was a pawn for the ruthless Mafia death machine known as *Murder Incorporated* without ever have bloodying his hands as gangsters murdered gangsters, to being a man who legally pulled the trigger on innocent victims. Three, to be precise.

While the ghosts that had appeared on those steps in Manila what felt like decades, and at times moments, ago would forever haunt his dreams making peaceful sleep non-existent, and tiny faces with a small, round, red epitaph of Manchurian life would forever remain in his daily vision, he was now back in the City of Brotherly Love.

For months to come the front pages of Philadelphia's newspapers would depict the horrors of Nagasaki and Hiroshima, yet he was unaware how easily the pictures could have been of San Francisco, New York, or...Philadelphia.

It was the city where he began as a teenage bartender at a tavern whose owner was *associated* with organized crime. He would learn that organized crime was the Mafia. He was *asked* to deliver packets of information to select patrons of the bar from the owner. He would learn that those "packets of information" came from the man *associated* with organized crime, *associated* with the Mafia, who was then *associated* with *Murder Incorporated.* He would learn that the patrons he passed information to were hired killers. He would learn that for a brief moment he held the life—or death—of another person in his hand.

He went from being a pawn—a courier, *associated* with *Murder Incorporated* where his secrets would remain hidden as he moved up the ladder to becoming the bag man responsible for picking up cash at the "gambling establishments" of the bar's owner, the man *associated* with organized crime, *associated* with the mafia, *associated* with *Murder Incorporated.*

Who actually signed his paychecks? Who was his employer? What happened when...? Answers to questions you already knew didn't need to be spoken out loud. Answers, which revealed or discovered, would never be shared. With anyone. Maybe the questions were meaningless if you didn't ponder the answers.

In the City of Brotherly Love he immediately went to see his wife, who immediately told him she wanted a divorce. Who told him his two sons were staying with her and that he would be financially responsible, *now get out*. Welcome back from the war.

George knew that he had to leave town, he had to get away from his soon to be ex-wife and all the rage and lord knew what fabrications she would throw at him. He also knew that if you were going to leave town you didn't tell anyone so they couldn't stop you.

He ended up in Chicago where on an unspecific afternoon only a couple of months after he had arrived he was approached by two FBI men who were sent to apprehend a "deadbeat father" that ran out on paying child support. Nothing could be further from the truth. He had never, would never, be a single day late in sending money for the welfare of his children. The FBI wanted to send him back to Philadelphia, which was now really lacking in the brotherly love department for George, to stand trial.

Afraid of what his ex-wife could have waiting for him in Philadelphia or even the gossip that could arise in *certain circles* from him being on a witness stand after being *escorted by the FBI*, he requested to be tried in Chicago.

Distance from his wife could be understood, it is questionable as to whether distance made a difference in *certain circles*. Actually, it wasn't questionable.

It took more time to go up the court house steps than for George to prove his innocence with receipts for every monthly payment of support that he had made.

With the trial behind him and a few more months of boredom in a city which he had literally grown to hate, George decided it was time for him to head home, back to Philly.

He had not been back a year from a war where his efforts had directly altered the course of world history, when his feet were once again pounding the pavement. Like many, on a cold winter evening he stopped at a bar only to look across the room and hope that his face was hidden behind the clouds of smoke as he looked into eyes that he was hoping to never see again.

It had been a night shortly before the war when George and a friend of his had been out drinking where they had met a couple of girls "out for a good time." They took them back to the two rooms they had in a nearby motel and only minutes after George had closed his door and the girl was doing her version of a strip tease, there was a pounding at the door. He opened it to two charging heads leading the bodies of Olympian rhinoceroses who wanted money – *now* – they could have said they were owed it for the girl in George's room, they didn't bother with pleasantries, they wanted cash.

He had fallen for one of the oldest tricks in the book; he was scammed by a girl who got him back to his motel room, only to be threatened into giving money to her goons.

Instinctively, he attacked the first guy who had come through the door with his concrete head targeting directly for his nose and started pounding fists into him. Before the guy hit the floor George's friend, hearing the fight, came rushing in from his room and grabbed the second ape before he had a chance to jump George from behind. George was pummeling the guy on the floor, taking out so much frustration that his friend had to lift him off the guy while there was still anything left of the bloody mess at his feet and then threw both of them out of the room – with the girls running behind – or maybe in front – of them.

His hands shook that night at the *type of man* he had just bloodied.

That monster was now sitting across the bar from him with every bit as much as much muscle as he had on that night in the motel room…and most likely some additional muscle attached to his hip.

George rose from his seat to leave before what he knew would be coming should he be seen; you kick the crap out of a guy who thought he was unstoppable and he would come back at you with a vengeance. He had been in the wrong place at the wrong time on too many occasions; he *was not* looking for another fight. Even if he won. With a broken beer bottle by his side he left the bar under the eyes of many, but not the ones who counted most.

The next day George went back to his old bartending job with the same *associated* guy. The guy hadn't changed but things had. *Murder Incorporated* was no longer operating and the owner had progressed from running gambling outfits to the fine art of counterfeit money.

There was no place better than a bar to launder money. No one fit to do it better than a bartender…a trusted bartender who knew who, and what, he worked for. The amount of cash that passed through his hands—as well as the small amounts that remained stuck to them, on any given night surpassed the salaries of all men in the bar combined.

It wasn't more than a few months before his boss brought him into the back room for a talk. This man, who was now speaking to him almost fatherly, told him that there were some major changes coming soon, changes by the *associated* and some new *unassociated* men. While he felt secure (as one can be) that he could whether out any storm that was approaching, he didn't think George could survive the upcoming shake up in the *organization*.

In any war, the foot soldiers (and Lieutenants) are the first to suffer. George had been through war, he knew when to retreat.

He was also smart, smart enough to know that any misinformation you could field to those looking for you, the safer you were. That was in principle, if they wanted to find you they would. He should know best. He had been the one responsible for passing along detailed information on targets who had no idea that their lives fit on a piece of paper.

To the customers in Philly his accent was southern, that meant he was from Texas, especially when you combined the accent with "the size that a man from Texas" was supposed to be. For ages they had been calling him "Tex" so when it was time for George to leave he simply told everyone he was going home and let them assume what they would. If anyone wanted to look for him they could start in Texas. It was a big state.

George wasn't lying, he did go home. Just not to Texas but to North Carolina.

Not that he would need it in the rural mountains of North Carolina, but he went back with a new suit, an *extremely ironic reminder* of his days behind the bar. He had gone shopping one afternoon for a new suit with two one hundred dollar bills in his pocket; one fake and one real. Why else buy a new suit? When he purchased his suit he paid for it with the counterfeit bill, or so he thought. Out on

the street he realized he had screwed up and was now the proud owner of a new suit that he didn't actually need and a bogus bill that he didn't want. Fate…or karma?

In 1948 George Wilson was back in the county where he had gown up, having grown up *far* more than anyone realized.

The Mafia, *Murder Incorporated*, illegal gambling, counterfeit money…it was good to be going home at the old age of twenty-seven. Oh yeah, that thing with Heavy Water too.

Chapter Eleven

"Home is the place where, when you have to go there,
They have to take you in."
~Robert Frost~

It is said that you can never go home again, but what if you left home and it never left you?

In 1948 George planted his size twelve feet back in the state that had bred them. In the time it took for the dust to settle after his feet hit the city center the roots dug in as they became part of his new home, Weaverville, North Carolina. The fortunate inhabitants of Weaverville, about ten miles north of Asheville and ten south of Marshall, where strong traditions of education, religion, and family values formed the foundations of this close knit community of *nearly fifteen hundred* residents, considered Main Street to be the *front gathering parlor* for the entire town. A town, depending on what a community of 1500 is called, that was one large home for all who had the pleasure to live there.

Coming from Philadelphia where 1500 people seemed to knock into you on a sidewalk as they hurried to places they had forgotten since breakfast, let alone comprise an

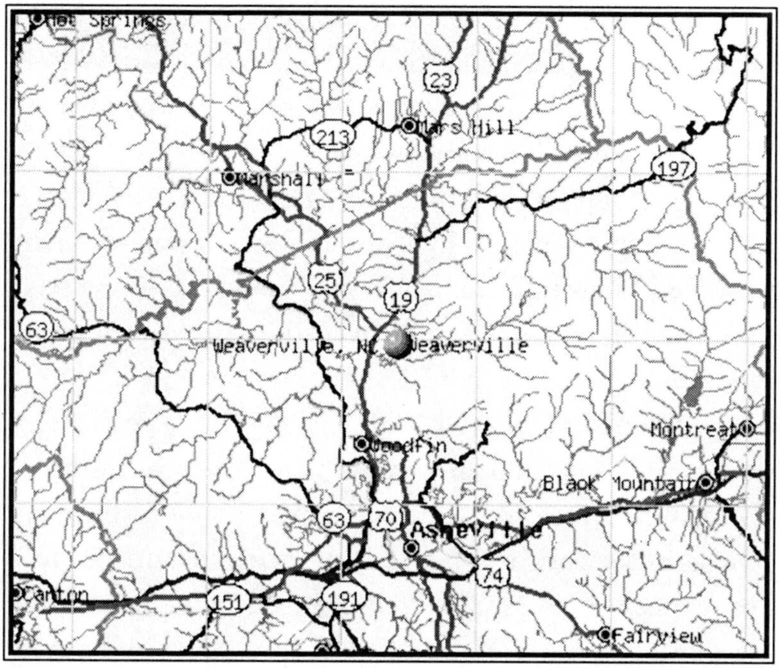

entire town, George welcomed the friendly waves from all he passed as they remembered the name of one of their own.

You can go home.

In ten years of absence he had been in circumstances that most men could never fathom. Yet, throughout that decade, regardless of the men he was associated with or the situations he found himself in, the goodness - the moral fibers that had been instilled in him as a child in these rural mountains had remained as the person in the mirror.

In a plaid shirt on Main Street you couldn't tell him or his welcoming hello from any other of the town's citizens, except for his size, baritone voice, and capturing eyes that is.

He took the town in, breathing the fresh country air that he had craved, knowing that he was home. He, George Wilson, was now standing in the place where his heart and mind had been for the last ten years.

The city attire and the mannerisms that came with it were quickly replaced by jeans and work boots when he decided to go into the profession he loved. Along with his brother, who lived in Weaverville, George was going to open an auto mechanics shop. Destiny.

Of course, along with dreams came the realities of opening a small business which, for George, proved a little harder than for some. He had no credit history and not a lot of cash to open a bank account and set up a business. *Legitimate cash that is.* He had left Philadelphia with $30,000 in counterfeit twenty dollar bills that he had *accumulated* slowly over the course of many nights. Where does one life end and another begin?

Unlike many who fell victim to the temptations of greed and flaunted "their wealth," he took precautions and only put small amounts of the counterfeit dollars in the bank at a time; just enough to fund operations in the beginning without raising any red flags. *Savings*, if you will. The business was doing well, but even on weeks when it wasn't and bills couldn't be met George subsidized the income from his *savings*, again being careful to deposit just the minimum amount of twenties he needed for the week; twenty dollar bills that he oiled and dirtied in the back room before depositing them for laundering. Not all terms come from a Latin root.

As ironic as it sounds, the scheme with counterfeit tender was the complete opposite to the George who would help people who were in dire situations by having them pay for his services with *what* they could afford, *when* they could afford it. Maybe that was why he had to use his own *savings*; to help people in need. On the streets of Weaverville you would see people go off to work or to the market in cars that didn't have a prayer if it wasn't for George, yet you never saw him in so much as a new pair of work boots.

The opposite side, or the real side?

By 1960 the automobile industry was booming and Weaverville had increased in population by at least an *overwhelming* hundred, although how many of those owned cars was debatable. And how many owned cars in need of repair created an even further paradox.

George had spent the past decade as the man he was always meant to be, in fact the man he always was. A corner of his mind would always be locked in on the past and he would never forget the people who would surely *never* forget him, but he had returned to what had never left him.

He had survived.

...*New Years Eve 1961*...It was a year when the threat of communism sent the world into frenzy, when John Kennedy took responsibility for The Bay of Pigs, and the erection of the Berlin Wall began. It was the year when within the DMZ of Korea that snipers who had never fired a weapon before were on alert for the enemy and a year when masses in Brussels were hording rations sure that the world was about to embark on another epic war.

It was the year George Wilson, all 6' 3" of him, walked into a bar on New Year's Eve in Asheville, North Carolina.

This is where *my* story begins.

Chapter Twelve

"Love is rarer than genius itself.
And friendship is rarer than love."
~ Charles Peguy ~

You grow up begging for food, always knowing the meaning of what it feels like to be hungry, it is a feeling that stays with you throughout your life. It is a feeling, a sensation, which stays at the core of your being and can either propel you in life or imprison you. Circumstances might alter, but the decision is yours.

It is not the desire for physical nourishment which can imprison you, but the acceptance of it. The acceptance of that that is all that life has to offer. Growing up on the streets of North Carolina in the 1930's I knew the effects of hunger everyday. It is not the conscious feeling of emptiness in my stomach that filled my mind, but the subconscious gnawing of knowing that I never wanted to go hungry in life. It is a far more powerful mantra than the thoughts of going hungry for a day. If anything, the latter becomes only an obstacle to the former, not the result. One leaves you cemented in hopelessness. One opens the path to the future.

I knew I was going to have a future. Stale bread today did not mean staler bread tomorrow, if *I* didn't let it. Although the fates were stacked against me, and in a way it is irrelevant to dwell on the misfortunes I faced as a youth as what remained within me was far more important, I did not for a moment give up on the morals and values I knew to be right. I did not let spending my pre-teen/early-teen years in a boys' home deter me from education. I did not let *me* stop *me*. For many years following it would have been very easy to do, far easier than fighting against the roadblocks that blindsided me. But I wanted more. More is a good motivation.

Materialistically wanting more meant a career where the only limitations I would face would be those that I could impose upon myself. Yes, a classified ad: motivationally orientated, self starter, people person, unlimited potential. I went into sales. When I was discharged from the army after the Korean Conflict I became, to those of you who are old enough to remember, the annoying person in a polyester suit who knocked on your door to sell you aluminum siding while you were watching *As the World Turns*. As an aside, you should have bought it; your house would still look good, and close your robe before you answer the door. After a couple of other endeavors in 1960 I managed to become a sales rep for the *Henley Paper Company* based in Asheville and one of the largest suppliers to printers, industrial accounts, etc. in the region.

This is important. 1960 comes before 1961 which brings me to New Year's Eve 1961, which I think I've accomplished rather quickly.

On that night, where it was still early enough to know for sure what I was seeing, I saw my friend "Tony" who owned a bail bonds business (which I didn't know until years later would become the catalyst to a friendship without definition to a man without definition) making his way through the room. He was next to (if he had been behind he would have been hidden from my view) a man who a bunch of men—who would never admit to being on their fifth drink while ice cubes flew from their glass, actually moved aside—as if they had a choice, to let him by.

George Wilson had a handshake that one did not expect from a man of his size. Although it never occurred to me at the time, there was a friendliness, a kindness if you will, that was there in this mammoth paw of his. In all honesty, I was more concerned with the bourbon in my other paw. Truth be told, I was ambidextrous at that point in my life. I could drink out of either hand.

At that moment I should have known that his handshake was anything but the handshake of a diplomat; it would be but one of the very many lessons I was to learn. To George, a diplomat—from the handshake to the smile, was someone who would pat you on the back and piss on your leg at the same time. George was *not* a diplomat. I should have been listening to his eyes instead of the breasts of the girl three stools away.

I was pretty astonished when he stopped by my house a week later as I was preparing to make my big move to the land of sunshine, mansions, and movie stars, as it has been described by *some other country folk who moved to Califorin –I-A*. He knew I was leaving and stopped by to check out my car for me. Really, that was it, "nice meeting you last week, how you doing, and I thought I would check out your car to make sure you don't have any problems on your drive." That should have told me all I needed to know about him.

Conversation was natural as if we had known each other for years. I am not sure if any neighboring kids rode their bikes slowly that afternoon to hear (and if they did, they still *are* hearing) George's monotone, funny laugh; hard to describe, sort of like a deep, cavernous "Huh," followed by a few more "Huhs" in between breaths that in the oddest way was as genuine as the smile on his face as it was hysterical to listen to. Or, it might have just been hearing baritone laughter coming out of a guy that could have checked under my chassis without needing a winch. It was infectious too, not the "huh" but the mood.

At the onset we found a common passion—an addiction to girls, or, as Elvis would put it, "Nothing but a hound dog." It was awful; he had the capability of making me feel celibate.

Drinking a couple of beers and bullshitting about hot girls, and here was this guy who I barley knew taking the time to make sure I would be safe. It was even stranger that he would take the time to come and talk to someone he just met knowing I was leaving the state. At the time I didn't know George hadn't come by to say goodbye, but to say hello. There is a big difference.

During that visit I was looking up to George because it was the only way to see him; in a few years I would be looking up to George in far more important ways. Maybe I already was.

In my "mechanically sound" car I left North Carolina for my exciting "Route 66" (not accurate, but idyllic) adventure only to have it turn into being a hellish trip across the country where it was so damn hot (hellish) that I was forced to sleep during the day and drive at night. Not a trip to write about. You're welcome.

Thing is, I actually thought about George a lot on that trip; with no idea why.

I spent the next two years in California working as paper rep for *Kimberly Clark* with the most memorable thing being that I can even remember so many of those boozing, partying nights.

Throughout those two years I was in touch with George through letters and occasional phone calls. Each communication seemed to bond our friendship as if it wasn't based solely upon a day bullshitting in my garage or hindered by three thousand miles. We became really close friends, closer than any friend I had ever had, and he probably knew it from the night we met trying to be heard over the ten second countdown.

I hadn't had known that it took merely a moment for George to completely analyze people. He could observe you in the mirror over a bar and know whether there was a foundation underneath worth inspecting or a catastrophe worth avoiding. In his "previous line of work" instant awareness of those around him could mean life or death. It is no wonder it became a subconscious habit within him to study, to predict, and to anticipate every individual within his radius; front, peripheral…and back.

Years later, and months too late, he would warn me to always assume anyone I met was a lying son of a bitch until they proved otherwise. I do not know how, or even *if* I was worthy, of meeting the requirements that George set down for people; let alone what took him moments to grasp in eyes that New Year's night which I am sure would wake up bloodshot.

Of course I had no idea at the time, but when George sought out your friendship it was an honor.

It was more than an honor. It was a merit badge you received *based* on merit.

In August of 1964, barely making ends meet and getting over a breakup, I received a call from "A.B.", an ex-girlfriend, yet very good friend, back in Asheville (for clarity sake I write Asheville, I was going to say home) who wanted to know if I would be coming home for a vacation. I didn't have money for gas let alone a vacation.

Is one to believe in miracles or the miracle of friendship?

She called me days later to tell me she was buying me a

round trip ticket and George wanted me to stay with him, with a car at my disposable of course.

I think the answer to the aforementioned question speaks for itself.

Booming auto industry or not, George had been forced to close his mechanics shop and now owned the *River Club*, a bar comprised of a rough crowd that he ran with an iron fist.

After only one week George asked me if I wanted to become a partner in his club. I thought it over while my eyes blinked. The chance to work with him at a place that would be filled with possibilities rather than daily headaches on the road dealing with stationary stores who needed envelopes; maybe my eyes didn't finish blinking.

I like to think George wanted to be in business with me, I also know that George believed that friends take care of each other. When one is hurting—in need of a job or a change in their life, a real friend makes that possible. It is not always about protection but sometimes precaution. Without a doubt I can say I didn't know any of this at the time. George didn't come with a manual. I always knew friends protect each other's backs. What I learned, or would learn, is that a true friend (if such a profound relationship can be reduced to a phrase) looks after the fronts too.

I returned to California and two weeks later—after borrowing money, returned a partner in the *River Club*. A week later George was informed by a sheriff he knew that the powers to be, with power being the key word, were going to shut him down. In a time when planting evidence of impropriety where none existed was a given rather than a veiled threat, rationalization was unnecessary, control was understood, and George was left with no options but to succumb to their power.

After only two weeks as a partner in my own business with a friend who had made it all possible the club was shut down.

I don't regret those two weeks or my decision for a minute. It brought me that much closer to a man I would soon never forget.

Chapter Thirteen

"Friendship is unnecessary, like philosophy, like art...
It has no survival value;
Rather it is one of those things that give value to survival."
~C.S. Lewis~

Those two weeks taught me something very important about myself. I had never liked sales as much as I thought I would. I truly appreciated the side of life that I was introduced to that catered to the building of strong business relationships fostered out of personal contact, but I didn't like driving through a sales territory that was the size of some obscure feuding country whose name would change every week or so depending upon which general currently had the largest *medal*, or hoping to get a lucrative territory that, while might be small in size yet not in prospects, is sated with sales reps who want nothing better than to stab the competition in the back. Or the front.

As much as I liked the financial potentials in sales, and I was more than willing to put in the work necessary to achieve the benefits, I didn't like the daily, hourly, headaches that came from dealing with potential customers who believed it was okay for them to raise prices while their supplier—me, was supposed to reduce costs. Not to mention the harassment from HQ to increase sales while HQ itself had no clue of their customer base.

The closing of the *River Club*, albeit rather quickly, made me realize I really liked working in a bar, and I was good at it. It wasn't that I merely related well with customers, I enjoyed being around so many people; *most* of them anyway. That brief period gave me the chance to utilize my sales and interpersonal knowledge first shown to me in the paper industry while giving me the taste for that elusive word *management*. I need to elaborate. It wasn't just the bar aspect of the job I liked, it was the hospitality industry as a whole.

Although I didn't know it at the time, I also had the best teacher anyone could have asked for.

George was as friendly as could be to customers, understood the habits and wants of his regulars and, at the same time, took no shit from anyone; the latter being something that would take me a *quite* a while to learn. It would take me even longer, two years according to my mentor, to learn the subtleties of doing it properly. To George it was simple and I reiterate out of necessity—or possibly to enforce the amount of times I needed to hear it before I understood the impact, the person in front of you was a son of a bitch until you figure out other wise. It sounds harsh. The truth often is.

I wish George could have had it on a t-shirt for me: "trust is earned by action, not a smile."

At the time I would have thought of it as a business mandate; later I learned the true meaning of his words. Saint

Thomas Aquinas once said, *"I would rather feel compassion than know the meaning of it."* In the world that George had let me into, not just business but more importantly friendship, it should have been phrased as, *"I would rather feel* Trust *than know the meaning of it."*

In a bar, especially one that catered to *certain* kinds of clientele, he knew that the smile on the guy's face ordering meant nothing when you didn't know where his hands were…or where they had been…or where they were going.

Unfortunately, the same is true in friendship, or the guise of it.

With my *vast* amount of experience I got a job managing a motel in Asheville owned by a successful attorney and professional gambler. I should have hightailed it right then and there. I rented rooms, acted as a caretaker and, although this was not on the want ad, ran the gambling operations of this "respected officer of the court."

Earlier I mentioned something about the definition of a diplomat, or was it about someone being a son of a bitch until they proved otherwise, or was it that I fell for the smile of an attorney without knowing that there was more to trust in a jack-o'-lantern's two toothed smile than in his?

George could have used this guy on a poster. It took me a long, long time to learn so many of the things George wanted to teach me from the moment I met him. As with most pupils, I had been oblivious to the practical assuming it was philosophical. I really would have preferred to learn without learning from my own mistakes.

In May of 1965, after having worked for this *gentleman* for only a few months, I told him I couldn't take it anymore.

I returned to my parents' home in New Port News and an ad in a Sunday newspaper set my future for the next two years. A club in Norfolk, Virginia was looking for a manager. Before I even met with them I should have thought about Norfolk; a sailor's home when he was not at sea, and when a sailor wasn't at sea that meant drinking and girls… and drinking. To put it bluntly, Norfolk was notorious for its sailor bars, places where "respectable" folks didn't go and where seamen ashore were known as marauding hordes out to get drunk, start fights, wreck property and "despoil women folk." On a good night that is.

Needless to say, this was not in the ad or in the eyes of the beautiful, actually foxy would be more descriptive, manger that hired me. To say I wanted that woman from day one would be putting it far too mildly. And George I apologize, I know I shouldn't have been thinking about shacking up with her or all of the *many* hot girls that worked at the club, and yes, management doesn't mix with the help, you shouldn't shit where you eat, girls still have to work after you screw them, and all of that other wonderful advice, but I did have an excuse that cannot be debated. I was a man.

Somehow it didn't matter to me that a girl could work there for two weeks and still not know which glass to put a Coke into…when she was *leaning* over the glass that is. Actually, I have no need to apologize. I did take his advice, but that didn't stop me from thinking about it.

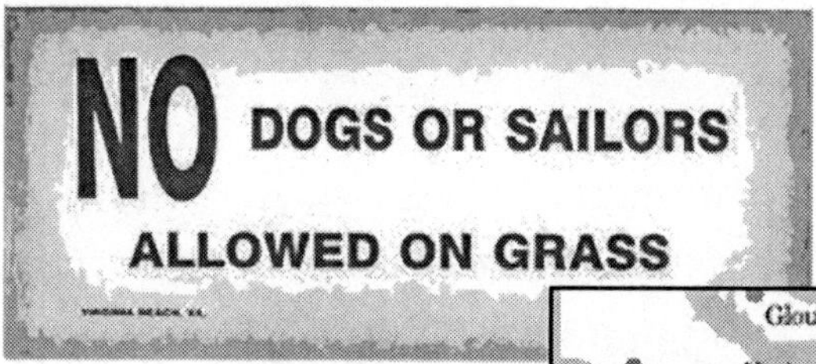

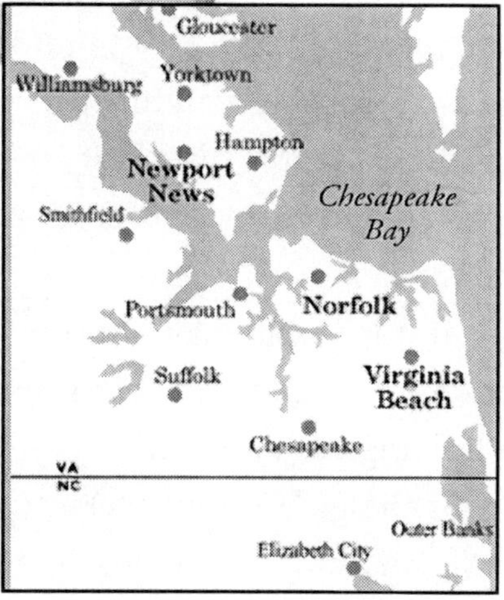

To put it bluntly, the girls who worked in this bar or any of the other *high class* establishments where the sailors felt compelled to make mobs at a soccer match look tame, were not exactly your home town, virginal, cheerleaders no matter what story they concocted to get their *tip*. And if the story led to a pat on the ass, just a pat mind you, than that meant a bigger tip as well. And yes Johnny, Scot, Rich, and Mark I'll be waiting for you when you get back from sea as opposed to hitting the streets looking for Andy, Tom, Dick, and Harry.

In 1966, where these girls in tight fitting outfits strutted far more than a smile as they hovered under purple lights to make them even more seductive and made a *hundred* dollars a night, *tips* is far from the appropriate word.

George was right, the cute girls were the business; the alcohol flowed all over the city. The bar with the best girls had the best beer; or didn't need it. It was not some cliché:

"Where the beer is cold and the women are hot." Not necessarily in that order.

I did make a grave mistake one night when George was in the bar. He saw me talking with a couple of girls trying to explain to them about protocol—I use that term loosely as they probably couldn't spell it let alone define it, and with his usual George like clarity told me I shouldn't be wasting my breath trying to talk sense to girls who only understood nonsense.

If it is possible for a fortune cookie to contain genuine, practical wisdom than he alone would have been considered a walking version of it.

If the girls were a stereotype—one that any man—excuse me, any *sailor*—would welcome, than "Marty", the owner, was the personification of a man who ran such establishments. You would never see him when he wasn't immaculate with a finely pressed suit and a tie that magically stopped 3.7 centimeters from his waist on all occasions. It was hard to tell which was shinier; his shoes or his slick backed hair. Slick being the appropriate adjective, and his office was the image of the man he wanted to portray complete with a large mahogany table—I think I missed the conference meetings, and a lounge chair that seemed to be screaming for a cigar. I should have known better.

I also should have known better about the *clientele*. I firmly believed in this venue of rock music, broken glasses, and scraping tables that I had become immune to, I could be nice to our *clientele*, tell them we all just needed to get along.

That lasted for the first few months. It then turned into a case of finding out if I could throw them out before they took a swing(s) at me or if I even gave them a chance to hit first. Some people collect matchbooks from a bar. I collected scars. I was the manager. It was my bar, my responsibility. If there was a problem I was going to fix it.

In other words - *jackass.*

It all changed one night when "Marty" took me into the backroom and instead of a lecture he wanted to know if I understood that he hired me to be the manager not a bouncer. I think the "*jackass*" thing sums it up pretty quickly.

That night made the difference. It was no longer a case of "me against them" but rather them against the shore patrol or the local authorities. If you broke a glass you were going to pay for it and while I was telling them this I had one of the girls get the shore patrol so that no matter what happened, how irate the testosterone filled drunk became, I would not be the one ending up with another scar. I let the police earn their paycheck as I readily gave up my position as a "*jackass*" who wouldn't take any crap without having to use my own fists to back it up…most of the time; it still was a bar. As an aside, fight with your back to the wall; no one can get you from behind.

It didn't occur to me until much later that the term "*jackass*" would be far too kind considering the mistake I was about to make, a mistake that had nothing to do with the *clientele*. Pardoning the redundancy, "mistake" also would be far too kind a word.

I was about to become "a piece of information" that could be scratched on one of *Murder Incorporated's* fact sheets should they ever need it. *Murder Incorporated* had long since dismantled, the Mafia hadn't.

"If they wanted to find you they would."

"Marty" always seemed to be aware of everything around him but not in a managerial sense but in a Gestapo sense. He would listen in on conversations where you would wonder whether if it was out of curiosity or paranoia. He even listened in on telephone conversations I had with George. At the time it meant nothing to me other than the nosiness of a boss.

Words come to mind to describe my actions that would have made the sailors blush.

Speaking with him afterwards about my conversations meant nothing to me, telling him about George meant nothing to me...telling him since he and George had both worked in Philadelphia that "Marty" should talk with George, see what they have in common, see if they knew any of the same people – all of this meant nothing to me.

Why should it?

It meant nothing to me when in 1967 completely fed up with the loud music, the fights, the income dropping, and the girls becoming less in abundance—and attractiveness, I left the club and moved back to Asheville.

It meant *a lot* to George. I just didn't know...yet. I didn't know that casual words had the potential to be a death sentence. Then again, I didn't know who, what, or why...yet.

Chapter Fourteen

"The glory of friendship is not the outstretched hand,
Nor the kindly smile, nor the joy of companionship;
It is the spiritual inspiration that comes to
one when he discovers that
Someone else believes in him and is willing to
Trust him with his friendship."
~Ralph Waldo Emerson~

I returned to Asheville with much the same feeling George must have had when he stepped into Weaverville almost twenty years ago. I was home. I had not led the dangerous life he had nor had I become a person who had an effect on the history of the world, but I was home.

Knowing I was staying with him upon my return, even at a point when our relationship hadn't been cemented like it would be, further fueled my emotions, increasing my sense of being home…with family. If I could have looked into the future I would have known how accurate that statement was when eventually his sons talked with me the way they talked with their father. In retrospect, it would be fair to say that since they had so much respect for their father, when they witnessed his confidence in me and our relationship together they in turn included me in *their* family in the way that only offspring can.

The only way this relationship of surrogate family built upon friendship can be truly understood is if you have experienced it; if you haven't, than you should wish you had.

As I sat in my car down the road from his house, I knew I was doing the right thing. It truly was a spectacular view. He had a simple three bedroom, what you would call middle class house but it resided on acreage of rolling green hills that in the winter seemed to be protected by snow capped mountains.

It was a setting engineered for serenity, a setting that welcomed peace rather than chaos, a setting where with any defile you would be affronting both the land itself and its creator; whatever you choose that word to mean.

I could see George standing in front of the house as I drove up. At forty-six he still had a physique that could make men half his age jealous and, on more than one occasion, make girls half his age available; both qualities which I envied – without admitting of course. The smile on his face said it all; he had that very rare look of genuine happiness, or an even better word, contentment.

Even from thirty yards away the smile told a lot about George. It, like George, was filled with a humor that always seemed to make people laugh. More importantly, it somehow made you feel better about yourself just by being with him. You were never quite sure if it was his jokes that were funny or if it was merely that you were happy to be around him and his good nature. Happy doesn't give the sentiment justice. It was more of a privilege.

He had a gift. He could bring out the best in people… when he wanted to…which was all he ever really wanted to do regardless of what he might have been forced to do. The man was blessed with a big heart which, I say with a big heart for him, turned out to be his ironic demise. And now he was standing yards from me.

I should have been skeptical. I knew it happened a couple of years ago and I had actually seen the vision before, but something about now seeing the reality in front of his house should have made me weary; George Wilson leaning on a sedan instead of a pick-up? Just not natural, but there he was all six foot plus of him welcoming me not as a houseguest but a member of his home.

For a moment it brought back the memory of him checking out my car before I left for California and, sanding in front of me, I would have bet my wallet that he would still have had no problem lifting up the chassis of his sedan.

By this point George was working for *Hunter Engineering* (hence the sedan) which specialized in the development of innovative products to serve the booming automobile industry during the 1960's. Unquestionably, *Hunter* was the undercar service leader by being the sole supplier of *alignment* and *balancing* equipment for Ford Motor Company's manufacturing and service. George would travel throughout the Carolinas, Tennessee, and the surrounding region

responsible for installation and training. I am not really sure how his legs fit behind the wheel of a sedan.

I doubt it was the car or the job, but George had changed his overall image to reflect his personality; an upscale veneer with the finest clothes adding definition to the man he was. To the few of us lucky to have known him, the clothes were irrelevant to the man underneath. The same is true for *those* that were *unlucky* enough to know him.

Shortly after I arrived I could see how his image and instincts could at times come into conflict…for the better. He had been at a club in Asheville with a girl who was a close friend of both of ours when a drunk, one who would have made the sailors in Norfolk seem tame, not only tried to put repeated, lewd moves on our friend but followed her to the parking lot where he was forcing her into his car. George came running up and the guy pulled a switch blade on him.

I don't know if the image of the blade that could have

been on a friend's throat brought the horrors of Manila back into the forefront of his mind. I don't know if the image ever lived anywhere else.

George took his expensive overcoat, the one that didn't give a clue as to the person underneath, wrapped it around his arm in a manner few men would instinctively do, and stood up to the guy at which point the guy knew he was dealing with a pro—a seasoned fighter not to be messed with, and ran off. George was not merely left without having to dirty his cashmere, lamb's wool or whatever *GQ* garment he was wearing, but without having to unleash that which he vehemently tried to contain.

It was only a couple of weeks later that I mentioned to George about "Marty" and how I told "Marty" that it would have been great if they had had a chance to talk.

The announcement got me a stabbing look I didn't understand and frankly didn't question. One week later I found out the meaning behind the look and, slowly, answers to questions I didn't know I had.

Answers that frightened me as the "who, what, and how" that I was oblivious to slowly came into focus.

At the time I was far from understanding that the true value behind the answers lied not in their history but in the wisdom they had generated.

I also didn't know what I had done.

I'm not sure I wanted to.

We were sitting in George's living room when he told me about a friend of ours, astonishingly the friend who was with

George the night I had first seen him *all those years ago* on New Year's Eve 1961, and the trouble he was now in. "Tony" owned a bail bonds business. What I, or most for that matter, didn't really know was that the bail bond business, like the juke box industry, was run by the Mafia, with a capital "M." The capital "M" insinuating all that one associates with the Mafia that they hope isn't true...and pray never to see. When facing difficulty "Tony" had borrowed money from his "partners" and as George described his scenario to me it became the catalyst for him to start telling me about his life.

The entire time he was talking my mouth was...

...open.

Each segment of his life he shared with me either filled me with fear or admiration, amazement or respect, awe or... fear. With each story, each passing moment, and each bit of his life that he revealed our friendship grew into a bond that I had never experienced before, a bond that few individuals are fortunate to experience with another human being. I didn't contemplate it at the time, most likely because it had never happened, but when a man begins to open his life to you, to share experiences and lessons—both good and bad, it is the beginning of something so much stronger than friendship.

It is a friendship that is built on merit and trust, a friendship that leads to respect. And, if you are as lucky as the one in a million I am fortunate to be, a friendship that leads to the love of another human being.

George later told me that I knew more about him than any other person in the world. That one sentence says it all. It was not what I knew that made a difference in our friendship, but that he had confided in me. Only me.

When he explained in a voice so calm, so controlled that made it almost mystical, how you could never escape from the Mafia or *Murder Incorporated,* that he knew *first hand* how they tracked people's habits and locations, and it led to a life of him always being cautious and aware of his surroundings I could feel something twitch in my brain, a thought that I wasn't able to completely grasp yet knew it was there.

When I found out that no matter where he was going he never took the same route, always arrived early or late for an appointment to avoid predictability, and to that day slept with a forty-five on his pillow or on the seat next to him in the car I could feel the thought in my head scrambling to break free.

When he told me that when you are talking with someone you never know who they are, what they are hiding behind their mask, and what danger could be hidden in their background the thought was at the tip of my tongue.

When he told me days later about a phone call he got from his old boss, *the* boss, in *Philadelphia*, I was petrified when the thought that I had been trying to keep hidden instantly surfaced. *You never know for sure who you are talking to.* I should have known better.

I told "Marty" about George and him having been in

Philadelphia. Who knows what he "overheard" on the phone when we were talking or assumed even from glimpsing him in the bar, but he mentioned it to the people he knew back in the land of brotherly love. I had been clueless.

Although I wasn't in George's home on that night over twenty-five years after he had left *the life* behind when he received a phone call from Philadelphia, I feel as if I was. Although I wasn't in the room when he got that call, because of my stupidity with "Marty" I know how I would have felt. I think he knew who was on the other end before he picked up the phone. I could be guessing; it is the only way to remember a call that I knew I was responsible for.

First "Tony", then the Mafia and *Murder Incorporated,* then "Marty"... everything he told me came together.

When he told me that when you are talking with someone you never know who they are, what they are hiding behind their mask, and what danger could be hidden in their background was he talking about "Marty" or...himself?

Even though George always hoped his ghost was thought to be in *Texas,* to those that mattered he knew that a call could come at any time. He told me about their words rather pragmatically: "*We just want to let you know we know where you are.*" Translation, "*Keep your mouth shut.*"

I never asked him what he knew, what it was that had happened twenty-five years ago that was *not* among the many secrets he told me, that he needed to—had to, keep his mouth shut about. It didn't matter.

By the end of '67 I had begun working as a bartender

doing the winter- summer circuit; winters in Florida, summers in the north and in-between I would stay with George.

I would travel with him helping install equipment, not talking about his past, but trying to absorb the wisdom very few men ever learn that he was sharing with me. Wisdom about humanity and life that was far superior to any knowledge I could have acquired, if anyone was capable of teaching it, in any classroom.

It was the wisdom that children learn from…someone else.

While there was a side of George that was filled with danger and anger, it was a controlled anger…out of fear for himself and others. Sometimes the anger had not been in control. And…

…There was a side of George that knew if a person needed to be killed you killed them before they killed you. Whether I inferred the meaning of the words and the magnitude of the message without the implication of what he might have meant was irrelevant compared to the stories that I was soon to learn. Stories, brief flashes of light and darkness in a life filled with adventures and misadventures that were beyond comprehension.

A life, and at times death, that was entangled in the blood of a basement bar in Manila, a hut in Manchuria, a car in Philadelphia—how he deemed it unnecessary in this instance not to kill those who were going to kill him is beyond me, or the untold stories of life and death confrontations that I never would hear. It was a life governed with a pragmatic philosophy from a pragmatic man where the first part of the statement meant nothing without "before they killed you." And...

...There was a side of George that would go out of its way to help people without them ever being the wiser that he was helping them. Glory meant nothing to a man who had helped change the course of world history. And...

...There was a side of George that avoided conflict at all costs, but if it refused to avoid him it would be their loss not his. That is not to say that George didn't lose something, a part of himself, in all conflicts regardless of the outcome. And...

...There was a side of George that made him special. I lie. There wasn't a side that didn't.

It was December, 1971, almost ten years to the day we had met. George was taken, and with a man such as George *taken* is the only word one can use, from the world by a heart attack at the unforgiveable age of fifty. He wasn't supposed to leave me alone that soon.

At the time the only words I could manifest in-between tears was that he was a great man. It wasn't enough. There was more to be said that I couldn't get out.

At the time, maybe I didn't even know. I'm sure I didn't.

At the time, I didn't know what to share, let alone who to share it with.

At the time, I was selfish.

That was then, this is now, George was...

Epilogue

"George was what most young men would like to be when they grow up,
And wish they had been when they grow old."
~Roland Woody~

Books are like life. Sometimes the shortest ones possess the most meaning, have the truest soul, the biggest heart, and the greatest impact. Sometimes, life is like books. You want more pages.

At the age of thirty I met a man who over the next five years would become a close friend. By the time I was thirty-five, an age where given my lifestyle up to that point I would have considered middle age, I would say George was quickly becoming the closest friend I had ever had. Over the next two years I would say he was like a brother to me.

If brothers are as close as friends.

Over the next three years, less than 4% of my life as I now stand, I would get rid of the word "like."

On that day in December of 1971 when I was given the honor neither I nor anyone deserved of placing George Wilson's coffin upon my shoulder I was lying to myself that George was like or in any other way conceived a "brother" to me.

I lied for the next forty years.

In retrospect it wasn't so much a lie as a feeling without definition. A feeling, a relationship, that having never experienced I couldn't put the appropriate title to, if in fact a title is necessary to something you feel in the depth of your soul. George Wilson was what every boy craves and every man fails to treasure until it is too late.

George Wilson was an older brother to me. The older brother that is seen in films that in our hearts we wish would exist.

He was the brother seen on screen that lets you follow him around because he wants you with him, not because he deems it necessary but because he values your companionship as much as you do his. When the tears aren't welling within me I can use the word "I" as opposed to "you."

As a child, he would be the older brother that protected you from the world.

As a man…he protected me from myself.

As a child, he would be the older brother that taught you about the world.

As a man…he taught me about the world.

The one part of the movie that strikes the chords of all those watching is how the child filled with idolic admiration, regardless of their age, wants to desperately be like their older sibling. In my case, life didn't imitate art. They were the same.

What he taught me about life and humanity, both the good and the bad, in the last thousand days of his life are paramount to an older brother teaching the kid he puts his arm around as he talks about girls. The feeling, the care, and concern are the same. The subjects are of a far greater magnitude.

It is okay for a man to say he loves his older brother.

When I was with George I respected and admired him from afar and when we were apart my respect and admiration were intimate. Men

People often say that brothers are on "the same page." I believe George allowed me to read over his shoulder. He was a man that went beyond influencing me but impacting me, guiding me, sharing not only the wisdom in his head but the warmth in his heart. It was a warmth, a genuine caring for his fellow man that those who knew him throughout Marshall, Weaverville, and all the surrounding towns would never forget. Those same folk who would never forget his tenderness would forever be incredulous of his past.

The past...where some he met incurred the antithesis to warmth. Once.

To spend your early adult life, at a time when today we consider twenty-one year olds to be kids, in the web of *Murder Incorporated* and the clutches of the Mafia is unfathomable to me. To have survived and changed is surreal. To be under their radar till the day you die is... believable.

George shared more with me than with any other individual. I cannot and do not want to know the secrets he took to his grave.

For me to be more enamored by the man I knew than by the actions of his life is…reverence.

Many of us, myself included, think our lives were hard, filled with insurmountable obstacles. George's life was not about the challenges, often life threatening circumstances that he encountered, but the way that a man survives.

With George Wilson survival pales in comparison to the quality of a person he became after each survival. It was a quality, a concern for another human being that he shared with all he came in contact with. *Almost all.*

I've stated that he changed the course of world history. Today, were it possible, he would have been the person to lie atop the World Trade Center to protect the people below.

For some of us history is relative while selfishness often reveals truth. It doesn't matter to me that George might have changed the course of events for the entire world that day before I was even driving. I was fifteen when the bombs exploded over Japan. That could have been over me. He changed *my* history.

I have been to the National Archives in Washington.

Manchuria, like all George told me, is true.

I never said thank you. To him and the seven who died on that mission.

If history does not repeat itself and man repeats history than I pray that I have repeated some of the history of

George's life by becoming even one percent of the man that George was.

There are certain clichés that are born out of absolute, irrevocable, truth. I am a better person for having known him. I wish I knew how good a person I could have become if I had known him longer.

I sit here now as I wish I could have stood forty years ago not to honor the most amazing man I have ever known but to say out loud, "I loved him. He was great man. Thank you for being my older brother. The one most only find in the movies."

"Ashes to Ashes, Dust to"

"Few of us write great novels; all of us live them."
~Mignon McLaughlin~

CPSIA information can be obtained at www.ICGtesting.com
Printed in the USA
LVOW081202150413

329133LV00001B/3/P

9 781614 931720